Tess Scholfield-Peters

Dear Mutzi

A heartfelt and beautifully written homage to Scholfield-Peters' forebears, who were caught in the 20th-century horrors of fascism and anti-semitism, and, in her loving portrait of her grandfather, to the survival of the human spirit. A moving contribution to the literature of the Shoah and its ricochet effect down the generations.

—Anna Funder

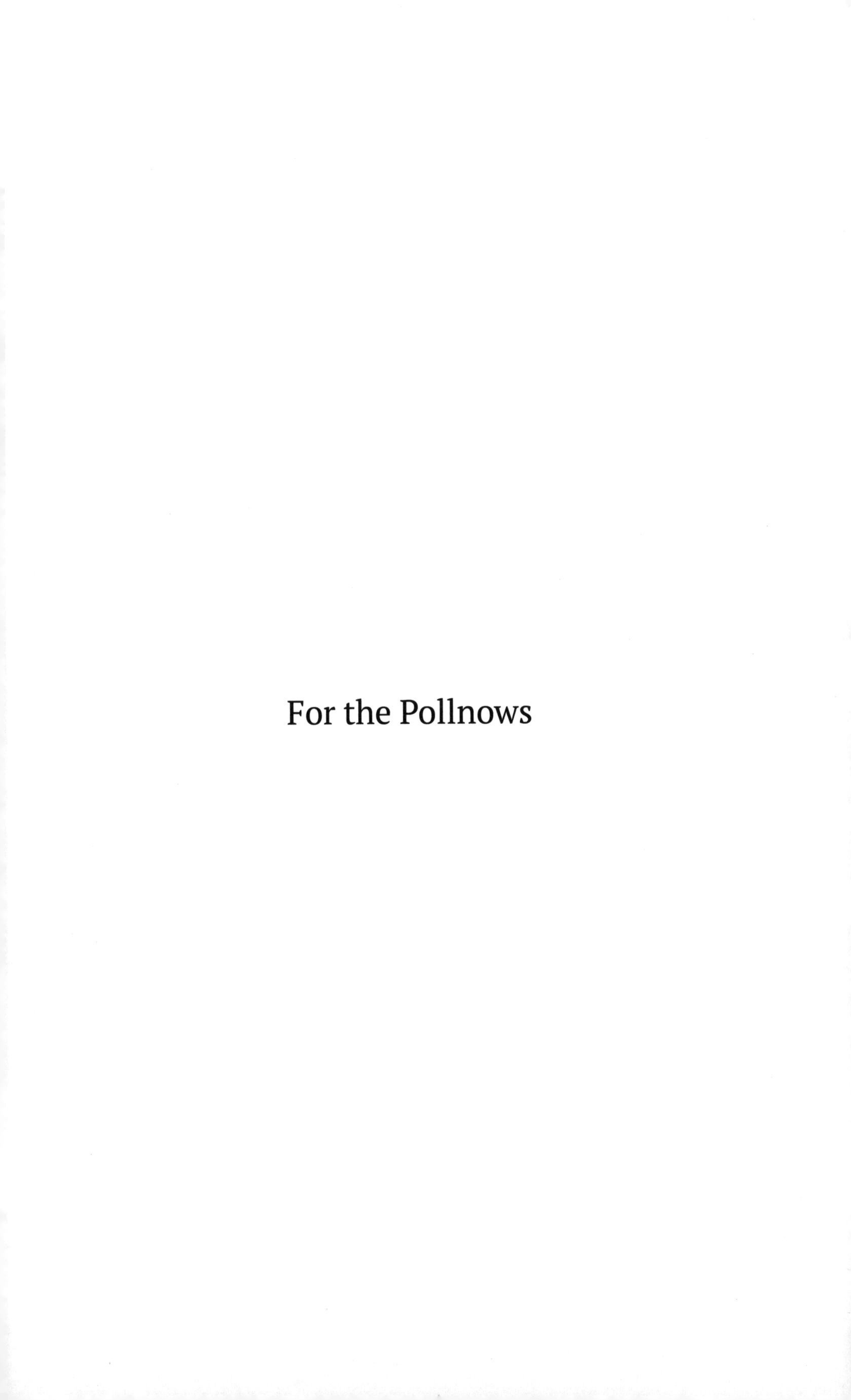

For the Pollnows

Author's note

This book is a reconstruction of my grandfather Harry's story, drawn from memories, letters and my own imagination.

This project began in 2019 when I happened upon a collection of letters written by Harry's parents, my great-grandparents Max and Edith Pollnow, two non-practising Jews from Berlin who perished in camps during World War II. Until that day, all I knew of Max and Edith was a handful of facts: where they lived and how they died—a tragic story, one of many millions from the Nazi genocide. In their letters I felt a pulse, and for the first time my sketchy imaginings of who these people might have been were transformed. Max and Edith stood before me: living, breathing people with hopes and sorrows and human intricacy. I felt compelled to take this remarkable, new feeling of acquaintance with the long dead, write it down and further it with research.

At the same time, Harry entered his 100th year of life. He began to recede into the early years that I was busily excavating. For every retrieved detail, countless lay buried. The impending grief of losing Harry and this history settled heavy in my chest during his last years, but still I asked questions, recorded our conversations, in the hope that we might bring his forgotten past back into the light together.

To tell this story, I draw from memories shared with me by Harry's partner, Lynn, and Harry's children: my mum, aunty and uncle. I draw from the countless conversations I have had with Harry over the years. I have interspersed Harry's recorded testimony from the University of Southern California (USC) Shoah Foundation's Survivors of the Shoah Project[3] and some of the many photographs he took as a teenager in the late 1930s. Every letter that appears in the text is real, translated from its original German, some condensed to only reveal information that pertains to this story. While all the main characters are real, some peripheral characters have been imagined but nonetheless derived from my research.

This reconstruction is one facet of a life that spanned an entire century. My grandfather was a different man to different people. In some ways he lived many different lives, and I only knew him during his last one. We did not have the close, playful relationship that many of my friends enjoyed with their grandparents. He never outwardly displayed affection beyond a salutatory peck on the cheek. But I revered Harry, and every word we exchanged was a gift. As dementia took hold of his final years, early memories stirred recognition in the increasingly distant present. These memories connected us, spurred our conversations, illuminated for me why Harry became the man that he was.

For many years, Harry was burdened by fierce anger, that of a man who had lost everything and experienced too much atrocity, much too young. He was a brilliant doctor, a true legend in the medical profession. He was a doting grandfather, adored by his family and friends. But before all that, he was Hermann Pollnow, the only child of Max and Edith, who called him Mutzi. I hope I have done justice to their story.

Since the days of the Bible, the destiny of many peoples has been to be driven from their homes and to wander over the face of the earth. From ancient times until today, displacement and, for some, resettlement, as a result of poverty or of political, racial and religious persecution, has been the lot of minorities in many parts of the world. Great political events and upheavals always leave in their wake the shattered lives of ordinary people, now refugees, homeless, on the move, with only one immediate desire and need: to survive.

We have become so used to the desperate plight and cry for help of millions that it is often a sheer impossibility to grasp the enormity of the human tragedies involved.

—Wolf Simon Matsdorf[1]

*

Place of birth remains place of birth, even when the names of the streets have been changed.

—A. Hirschberg[2]

The immediate Pollnow family

Hermann Pollnow, Harry's paternal grandfather

Caroline Samter, Harry's paternal grandmother

Dr Ludwig Pollack, Harry's maternal grandfather

Ella Jacoby (formerly Kempner and Pollack), Harry's maternal grandmother

Max Jacoby, Ella's second husband and Harry's step-grandfather

Hans Pollnow, Max's brother and Harry's uncle

Johanna Pollnow, Hans's wife and Harry's aunt

Dr Max Pollnow, Harry's father

Edith Pollnow, Harry's mother

Hermann Pollnow (Mutzi), Harry Peters, Max and Edith's son, my grandfather

The immediate Peters family

Harry Peters

Helen Peters (formerly Bridgefoot), Harry's wife

Lynn Rawlings, Harry's partner

Julia Peters, Harry's daughter, my mother

Cathy Peters, Harry's daughter

Lindsay Peters, Harry's son

1

Herr Waltbund, a small-framed man with polished shoes and a neatly clipped moustache, walked briskly along the busy Altonaer Strasse thoroughfare in central Berlin. On that spring day in 1930, the clouds in the sky were faint wisps against striking blue, and the trees that lined the Tiergarten were full and fragrant. The weather felt unseasonably warm. Waltbund carried a leather case for his scissors, curlers and brushes, which he clasped tightly in one hand, a lit cigarette in the other. He reached the corner of Lessingstrasse and Altonaer Strasse at 10.25, five minutes early. Waltbund sat his case by his feet and finished his cigarette, looking out over the main street. A packed tram groaned and hissed to a halt and a horde of smartly dressed passengers alighted, probably on their way to the park on such a fine morning. The skin beneath Waltbund's starched collar began to perspire. He trod on his cigarette and crossed the pavement to flat number 8. He paused at the door, wiped his brow and knocked.

'Yes?'

'Herr Waltbund for Frau Pollnow.'

The door opened to reveal a small woman in a white apron,

with two deep lines across her forehead and grey hair as thick as rope tied back in a braid.

'Good morning, Frau Warnke,' said Waltbund. 'It's a pleasure to see you.'

Frau Warnke's expression softened. 'Good morning, Herr Waltbund,' she replied. 'Come in, please.'

Waltbund followed her down the narrow corridor and to the right. Further along was the entrance to the hospital owned by the Allgemeine Elektricitäts-Gesellschaft (AEG), one of Germany's largest industrial manufacturers. They allotted these adjoining flats to esteemed hospital staff, though the Pollnows' flat was far from ostentatious. In fact it was cramped and noisy, and the dust from the footpath settled much too comfortably on every sill and in every crevice of the place. The walls trembled each time a train roared past. Waltbund peered out of the living room window. He could see all the way across the Tiergarten's glittering canopy to the hazy outline of the city beyond. Frau Warnke cleared her throat.

'Herr Waltbund, Frau Pollnow is ready. She's in her bedroom, as usual. Would you like anything to drink?'

'Coffee, please, if you would be so kind.'

Frau Warnke nodded and disappeared into the kitchen. Waltbund went to the bedroom door and knocked.

'Come in, please,' came a soft, high-pitched voice from the other side of the door. Waltbund entered and saw Edith Pollnow sitting at her dressing table. She turned to him, smiling. She wore a pale pink dress and her dark hair was loose at her shoulders. On her wrist was a bracelet of grey pearls. Sitting behind Edith on the bed was a young boy Waltbund knew was her son, Hermann.

Hermann held a notebook and pen and was writing with fixed concentration.

'How are you, Frau Pollnow, my dear?' Waltbund took Edith's hand and shook it lightly.

'As well as I can be,' Edith replied, her smile slightly faded. 'Mutzi, say hello to Herr Waltbund.'

Hermann looked up from his notebook, only just noticing there was another person in the room. He stood up from the bed, clicked his heels together and bowed.

'Good morning, Herr Waltbund,' he said.

'Good morning. You get bigger each time I see you, Mutzi. What are you scribbling in that notebook of yours?'

'Mathematics, sir. My father gives me problems to solve while he's at work.'

'I see! How very industrious.'

Edith caught her son's eye and nodded, smiling.

Waltbund turned his attention to Edith.

'Now, what would you like me to do today?'

He clicked open his leather case and laid out his scissors and electric curling iron. Then he took Edith's hair in his hands and gently ran his fingers from her crown to her shoulders. Hermann watched his mother's reflection from behind his notebook. He watched as she turned her pale face slowly to one side then the other, drew her hands to her shoulders, curled a tendril around her index finger.

Hermann knew there was something wrong with his mother, but he did not know what. One day, he couldn't remember exactly when, Edith became tired. Hers was a tiredness that could not be cured by sleep or fresh air or food. Edith's tiredness was deep, beneath her bones, in her cells, Hermann heard his father say once. In Edith's reflection Hermann saw flickers of how she used to be, a trick of the light.

'A trim to this length'—she touched a few inches below her ear—'then a shape in the usual style.' Edith wore her hair curled and pinned back at the nape of her neck.

'Perfect,' said Waltbund as he picked up his scissors.

'Mutzi, tell Herr Waltbund about your studies,' Edith chirped.

'I'll be starting soon at Friedrich-Werdersches,' Hermann replied. Friedrich-Werdersches Gymnasium was a secondary school for students who wished to pursue medicine or law. They were taught Latin, Greek, classical German arts and culture—those prized aspects of education passed down from their fathers, and grandfathers before that.

'Ah, yes, of course. A good school, and quite close by. I suppose you want to be a surgeon like your father?'

At ten years old, Hermann hadn't given it much thought.

'Both Mutzi's grandfathers were doctors too, you know,' said Edith. 'My father used to own this hospital before he died.'

'Is that so? Well, you're a medical family, then.'

'Indeed,' said Edith. 'But you have plenty of time to decide what you want to do with your life,' she continued, catching Hermann's eye in the mirror reflection. Edith observed her son, the way he furrowed his brow and scrunched his hand into a fist around his pen, just like his father.

Frau Warnke came in with two porcelain cups of coffee and placed them down on the blond oak table by the dresser.

'Frau Pollnow, how are you feeling?' she asked.

'I feel well at the moment, thank you, if a little tired.'

'We're almost done, and then you can rest,' said Waltbund. He picked up his coffee and took a sip. Waltbund never asked what was wrong with Edith, that would be imprudent. But he had noticed changes in her, especially in the last few years. She moved slower these days, took much more care with each step. Since he'd known her, Edith had used a cane, but Waltbund now noticed her complete reliance on this aid. She seemed to struggle beneath her own weight.

'You know, I look forward to your visits immensely,' Edith said to Waltbund as he brushed the hair off her shoulders and switched off his curling iron.

'As do I, my dear,' he replied. 'Doesn't your mother look wonderful, Mutzi?'

Hermann nodded. 'Yes, she does.'

Edith beamed at the mirror. 'Much better, thank you.' She touched her hair lightly, tucking a strand behind her ear.

'You're very welcome.' Waltbund swept Edith's trimmed hair into a pile on the floor and picked it up in a small dustpan to discard. Then he clicked his case shut and turned to leave.

'You'll take good care of your mother, won't you, Mutzi?'

Hermann nodded.

Waltbund drained his coffee cup, shook Edith's hand, then Hermann's, and shut the bedroom door behind him.

Edith turned to Hermann.

'What are you doing today, Mutzilein? It's a beautiful day outside.'

'Alfred and I are going to the park and maybe the zoo.'

'How lovely. I wish I could come with you. We used to have so much fun at the zoo.'

'I'll tell you all about it when I get home.'

'I'd like that. Now, I think I might have a lie down. Help me to the lounge, please.'

Hermann helped Edith up from her chair, into the salon and onto the lounge. The window that looked out to the street was open. Hermann leaned out and watched the traffic congestion below. He spotted Alfred walking across the road.

'Close the window, please. The noise is too much.' Hermann did as he was told. Edith's eyes were closed.

'Alfred is downstairs, Mutti.'

'See you when you get home. Say hello to the lions for me.'

Alfred and his parents were good friends of the Pollnows. They lived only a ten-minute walk away on Agricolastrasse, across the Spree. Together the boys walked the short distance into the gardens, passing street vendors and the old man with his barrel organ. The old man had a front tooth missing and holes in his shoes, but turned the wheel of his tinny instrument as though it played the most beautiful melody in the world. Hermann and Alfred blocked their ears and quickened their pace towards the park. Once inside, the boys slowed, caught their breath and looked up to the whistling trees and the sky beyond. Soon they were lost in the park, running and climbing, and would be until the sun lengthened their shadows and tinged the leaves with the glow of evening.

My grandfather Harry rarely speaks of his mother, Edith. Or perhaps I should say Harry never freely offers any information about his mother, Edith—only when I ask: 'What was Edith like? What do you remember about your mother, Harry? What was she interested in? Can you remember anything at all?' I want Harry to brighten and say, 'Oh, yes, I remember it all! My mother was beautiful and kind, she loved the theatre and she loved to read, Goethe was her favourite, and Brecht second. She listened to opera records in the evenings with the windows closed so nobody heard. I remember the prickle of her perfume as it pinched my nose when she leaned down to kiss my cheek. I remember the exact moment I realised her health was declining, I saw the change in her complexion and her movement. I remember my parents' relationship changing as the pressure from a hostile Berlin made it impossible to live normally. Yes, I remember it all. Where would you like me to begin?'

Of course, Harry's memories of Edith are few, and such character-defining details I can only imagine. When I ask these questions, his usual answer is, 'My mother? She was very sick, always in bed.' Which is why I was dumbfounded when one afternoon not long ago, while we were sitting together, Harry said suddenly, as though he just remembered, that the night before he had dreamed of his mother. My heart raced.

'A dream, Harry? What did you dream?'

'Waltbund.'

'Waltbund?' I repeated. I'd never heard this name before. Harry's words unfolded. In the dream, Harry was a child on his mother's bed, looking at her reflection in the mirror while her hair was being styled by a man who, he very clearly remembered, was called Mr Waltbund.

'Waltbund,' said Harry. 'I can see him. He was a very nice

fellow. And my mother, sitting in front of her …' He motioned a straight line in front of him, his hand hovering from left to right as though the dream was appearing in front of him, an apparition.

'Dressing table?' I offered.

'Yeah, dressing table. I can see my mother sitting there, in front of her mirror.'

'Can you remember anything else about your mother?'

'No, that's all.'

It came to Harry in a dream, and yet this picture of Edith is the most vivid I have of her. Edith captured in a mirror reflection, through the eyes of my child grandfather. I caught a lucky glimpse before the window closed again. I keep this picture close, I colour its edges and restore it in places. I sit it next to another of Harry's timeworn memories: his childhood friend Alfred Gotthelf. I straighten Alfred's collared shirt and dust off his brown leather shoes. I bid farewell to the two young boys as they cross the street together, laughing and playing. I lose sight of them as they disappear between the trees and I return to the present.

Here is everything I know about the Pollnows.

Max's and Edith's lineages can be traced back to the early 1700s in Germany. Max was descended from the deep-rooted German-Jewish line of Phillip and Caroline Veit, whose marriage in 1796 began generations of German-Jewish upper- and middle-class families. One of these families was the Veit-Simon family, with whom the Pollnows had a close relationship in Berlin, along with the Rosenthal-Schneider family, also distant relations.

The families Veit-Simon, Rosenthal, Schneider and Pollnow had regular reunions, and the history and close ties of these families were important socially and culturally. Max Pollnow's grandparents were Friedricke Simon and Michael Samter; both were born and died in Berlin. Their daughter Caroline married Hermann Pollnow in Berlin in 1883, and Caroline and Hermann had two children: Max and Hans. Hans, Max's younger brother, married Johanna Horwitz, known as Anna, in Berlin in 1924.

Max Pollnow, Hermann's father and my great-grandfather, was born in Berlin on 5 June 1884. I don't know much about his childhood. Max's father was a surgeon too, and he grew up in the city so his younger years could probably be likened to his son's. Max attended Friedrich-Wilhelms University (now Humboldt University) in Berlin, and studied abroad in Zurich, then specialised in surgery. He became one of the pre-eminent surgeons in Berlin, and maintained that position for many years. At the outbreak of war in 1914, Max went to the Western Front. There he worked as a surgeon until the war's end in 1918. For his services to Germany, Max received an Iron Cross, the country's highest war honour. He never spoke of his time at the front to Hermann, or perhaps anyone.

Edith Pollack, Hermann's mother, was born in Glauchau, a small town in Saxony, to Dr Ludwig and Ella Pollack on 22 October 1894. It is likely that Edith and her parents moved to Berlin when Dr Pollack took up the position of medical director at the Sanatorium am Hansaplatz in 1906, when Edith was 11. The sanatorium was on the corner of Lessingstrasse and Altonaer Strasse and was commonly referred to as the Hansaklinik. During World War I, Edith worked as a nurse. Dr Pollack, Edith's father, died in 1920 and Ella, Edith's mother, took ownership of the Hansaklinik property. In 1926, Ella sold it to the Allgemeine Elektricitäts-Gesellschaft (AEG) when Hermann, her grandson, was six years old. The AEG employed Max Pollnow and he worked there as head of surgery until his expulsion in 1935.

Perhaps Max Pollnow knew Dr Pollack from the war, or perhaps they were already colleagues or associates in Berlin's medical community. It is likely that Max and Edith met through this connection, and were married soon afterwards in 1919. On 9 August 1920, Hermann Ludwig Pollnow was born, named after his two grandfathers.

Max and Edith first lived in the Hansaviertel district of Berlin, in a small flat connected to the hospital. The Pollnows were not wealthy; Max never owned a car or his own property despite his prominence in the medical community. The flat was right next to the train line, which muddied the air with soot and engine groans. In the early years of their marriage, Max and Edith went to extravagant parties and entertained colleagues from the hospital, family and friends, Jewish and non-Jewish, at their flat. Those early days of marriage were set against the backdrop of 1920s Berlin, before the cabarets were banned and certain pieces of art disappeared from gallery walls; before books were burnt. In those days, Max and Edith would have frequented the sprawling cafes on Kurfürstendamm, swum on Sundays at Wannsee and taken trips further afield to Italy and France. When Max and Edith took Hermann on holidays, they would go to Berchtesgaden, a village in the Bavarian Alps near the Austrian border, and stayed at a cottage owned by one of Max's patients near the Königssee (King's Lake). On weekends and holidays,

Hermann also travelled to the Veit-Simons' house, a sprawling villa in Dahlem, an outer suburb of Berlin, where he played with his cousins in the spacious gardens beneath the fruit trees. In the summertime, Hermann went with the Veit-Simons to the Nordsee resort in Duhnen, on a long stretch of beach on the North Sea, until the time when Jews were forbidden to holiday there.

Left to right: Edith Pollnow, Heinz Veit-Simon, Max Pollnow, Irmgard Veit-Simon. Date unknown.

Hermann was an only child with an ill mother and a father who worked from the early morning until very late in the evening. So, when Hermann was a young boy, most of his time was spent with the Pollnows' housekeeper, Frau Warnke, and his grandmother Ella. I believe Ella and Hermann were very close because in later years he spoke fondly of her, with more affection and detail than he afforded his mother. One of the vivid memories he shared was of the roast chicken that Ella would cook when Hermann visited her house on Sundays. Ella would take Hermann out to the cinema and buy him sweets and, later, cigarettes. In Ella I see a twinkle of mischief and playfulness, and warm maternity that Hermann remembered into old age. Ella's second husband was a solicitor and, interestingly, Hermann didn't like him. Perhaps he was strict and short-tempered, perhaps he was absent; I do not know why, but the care and warmth in his recollections of Ella did not extend to her second husband.

The Pollnows were German first and Jewish second. Their Jewishness was peripheral, observed only for the community's weddings and funerals. Were it not for the election of Hitler as chancellor in 1933, the Pollnows might have forgotten they were Jews altogether. The Pollnows subscribed to the community of German Jews who were indifferent to Zionism and enjoyed an assimilated metropolitan lifestyle, despite the increasingly hostile environment in which they found themselves. The Pollnow family had lived in Germany for centuries; it was unthinkable that, all of a sudden, they were no longer recognised as Germans. Hitler was a rogue, his supporters thugs and, to many Jews (the Pollnows included) he was just another in a long line of anti-Semitic politicians intent on ostracising them further from German life.

The Pollnows' living standard was slowly curtailed from 1933, when the racist Nuremberg Laws obstructed employment, income, education and most other essential facets of normal life for the Jewish community. Max was forced to resign from the AEG hospital in 1935 and move to another flat, in the Oberschöneweide district, because he was Jewish. He was only allowed to treat Jewish patients, which thwarted his capacity to earn a living. Edith was diagnosed with multiple sclerosis and pernicious anaemia and was soon confined to her bed. Hermann was expelled from Friedrich-Werdersches school in 1936 because he was Jewish. That same year, Berlin hosted the Olympics. As a teenager, Hermann was a skilled gymnast; his specialty was the parallel bars. Lynn, Hermann's partner, told me once that, years ago, he had mentioned in passing that he was part of the opening ceremony. I questioned this: a Jewish student part of the opening ceremony of Hitler's Olympics? But he was adamant, so I silenced my doubts.

Berlin's Altes Museum, taken by Hermann Pollnow. Date unknown.

*

Describe the social life at home.
We had a fairly close relationship. My parents entertained; they weren't well off. My father was never well off, he never owned a car. We lived in a unit, he lived in a unit all his life, never owned a house or anything like that.

Did they mix with Jews or non-Jews?
Mainly Jewish colleagues and friends. Some non-Jewish colleagues. Because I went to non-Jewish schools, I had quite a number of non-Jewish friends. And Jewish friends. It was a fairly, sort of, normal existence until the time it became rather, er, dicey.

What was the religious background of the family?
Ah, we were Jews. Liberal Jews. Not religious, didn't hold any of the High Holidays. Rarely went to the synagogue except for weddings and funerals.

What language did you speak in the house?
German.

Did you have any siblings?
No.

Tell me about your school life.
I went to preschool, I suppose, until I was eight or ten. Then went to a gymnasium, which was a humanistic gymnasium

specialising for pupils that intended to take up the professions like medicine or law. The languages were taught, Latin and Greek, mathematics, history. I stayed there, again, I was able to stay probably an extra year because of my father's war service.

Did you always want to be a doctor?
No, I don't think at that time I had any plans. Around 1936, it wasn't a question of what you wanted to do, it was more or less a question of what was best for oneself in, say, emigrating. That idea of medicine disappeared.

Did you ever experience anti-Semitism at school?
Minor. I never experienced any physical violence in the school. Many of my schoolmates were very supportive and, actually, until I left the school in 1936 or 1937, we had social intercourse, visited each other. I can't say that I experienced any rabid anti-Semitism. Some of the Jewish children that were in the school did experience discrimination and some also were physically assaulted. I was a pretty strong fellow at that time, I was a very good athlete and that counted quite highly with the Germans, especially gymnastics.

What sorts of things were you good at?
Parallel bars, mainly gymnastics, not so much athletics like running. I belonged to Jewish physical culture clubs.

What do you remember of the rise of Nazism?
Well, I remember the rallies. And the SA [Sturmabteilung] *stormtroopers marching through the streets of Berlin singing.*

I had non-Jewish friends of my father, who at that time, in 1933 and 1934, were still in charge of the hospital. One of the sisters there, her father was a big forester in an estate near Potsdam looking after game. A gamekeeper. I spent most of my holidays there. Her father was a member of the SA and took me to some of the rallies when Hitler spoke, near Potsdam.

Can you describe them for me? The rallies?
Well, they were exactly as you see them on television. Huge crowds, banners and people screaming for minutes and minutes. Giving the Hitler salute, inflammatory speeches by Hitler or Goebbels. It was as if people were completely mesmerised.

What sort of things were Hitler and Goebbels saying?
Well, I think that at that time, when I was 15 or 16, most of the things were pretty unintelligible to me. I was not politically aware of what was going on, as most Jews were not. It was a stirring sort of experience. Especially for young people to hear march music, all the banners, flags, drums and what have you.

Was it at that stage that you realised the danger for the Jews?
No. I don't think ... it's a very difficult question. Even today when I think about it, I'm not quite sure whether the Jews, my parents included, were actually aware of the danger. I remember a few comments, for example, 'We'll be alright', 'We're Germans', 'Fought in the war' and so forth.

Around this time did the attitude of your non-Jewish friends change towards you?

My personal friends from high school, their attitude didn't change. We never discussed, we didn't talk politics, that was very dangerous for them. But no, I must say that up until 1936 when I left, their attitude hadn't changed. Maybe they didn't, sort of, welcome me to visit them frequently, especially if somebody saw me ... But they came to my place and it was no hassle. But coming back to what the attitude was of the family with regard to danger, this subject wasn't discussed very much at home at all. There was never any discussion about emigration, my father wouldn't say, 'I think we have to get out, I have to try ...' that was never brought up. My sort of duty was to do my homework and don't get into trouble, and do what my parents wanted me to do. And they arranged, of course, for me to, later, when I had to leave school, to try first to learn Spanish and Spanish shorthand in case I should go to South America, so I went to a Jewish day school, which taught Spanish and Spanish shorthand typing. When that didn't come to any fruition, my father was put in contact with Gross Breesen, which was a training farm for young Jews. And I was accepted there, and as I was keen to take up agriculture or work on the land, that was quite acceptable to me.

Gross Breesen was a Jewish training farm not far from Breslau, in Silesia, which was anti-Zionist, completely anti-Zionist in persuasion, and trained people to go anywhere except Palestine.[4] *And, uh, I started there in about January or February 1938, and the leader in charge of the farm was Professor Bondy. We had lectures, seminars at night, everything was a bit German in the arts, German musicians, Beethoven and history. There was no Hebrew—I'm sorry, that's not right, we had service; Friday night we had a short Shabbat service, that was about all. Otherwise, the Jewishness wasn't stressed at all, much. It was run on fairly disciplinarian lines. We worked hard, just like farm labourers, more or less, and at night we had to change: white shirt, be tidy, dress up for dinner and so forth. There were boys and girls there, on that farm, that went on until 9 November 1938, when the Jewish man shot the German diplomat in Paris.*

At this time, 1938, the Jewish community was split between many complex paths of ideological thought. One was epitomised by the Centralverein deutscher Staatsbürger jüdischen Glaubens (C.V.), an organisation that advocated for the civil rights of German Jews.[5] The Pollnows shared the C.V.'s view that Jews were as much German as the Protestants and Catholics because, aside from the 2,000-year history of Jews in Germany, Judaism was a religion, not a people. In opposition to this were the Zionists, who rejected this assimilationist view, arguing that, as evidenced by the rise of Nazism, Jews would never be absolutely integrated into German society because, like Germany or Austria or France, the Jews were a nation in need of a rightful homeland, which they saw as Palestine.[6]

Along with thousands of other German-Jewish youths, Hermann was a member of a Jewish cultural club, part of the wider Jewish youth movement, specifically the conservative Schwarzes Fähnlein[7] or Black Squad. This group shared the same ideology as the Jewish 'assimilationists' in their appreciation of both Jewish and German arts and culture. The movement believed in the collectivisation of young Jews and fostering of Jewish self-awareness, to be consciously Jewish and German. Three key concepts were propagated across the youth group movement, which also comprised the Zionists: *Gemeinschaft* (community); *Haltung* (deportment and attitude); and *Lernen* (learning).[8] These concepts were put into practice through group activities. The Jewish youths went hiking and camping, spoke about philosophy and morality and valued athleticism and community service—all with the aim of producing improved and self-actualised young Jews who, they believed, rightfully belonged in German society. The ideologies, teachings and community spirit of the Bund youth movement, as well as the disinclination to emigrate to Palestine, laid the foundations for the Gross Breesen agricultural training school, which Hermann attended from January to November 1938.

Gross Breesen students were predominantly from Jewish urban middle-class backgrounds. They no longer had education prospects in the cities but had an urgent need to become skilled in the face of emigration. Gross Breesen was nearly 400 kilometres from Berlin, on the border of Germany and Poland in an area once called Silesia. It was a non-Zionist training farm for Jewish youth, which prepared its students to emigrate to countries other than Palestine: England, North and South America, Africa and Australia. Training farms were increasingly popular among young Jews because regular schooling had ceased and emigration had shifted from an outlandish idea to probable reality; skilled emigrants had more of a chance at obtaining visas. The overseer of the school was Professor Curt Bondy, a renowned psychologist and educator.

Bondy was a strict man who ran the school with merciless discipline. He believed, right to his core, that his students, the Gross Breeseners, were to have their sense of self restored and sense of community fortified through manual labour and his own teaching. These young students had internalised years of hatred and the belief, proliferated by their fellow countrymen and women, that they were subhuman. What relief, then, what good fortune, to find themselves at Gross Breesen, away from harm, far from violence, allowed to learn again, to play music again, to perform, to read Mann, Hofmannsthal, Schiller and Zweig. Free to study the prophets Amos and Isaiah, to recite Hebrew prayers. How wonderful it was to wander by the lake and lie beneath the oak trees, to feel sore muscles at the end of the day; to be given purpose.

The Gross Breesen Schloss,
taken by Hermann Pollnow, c.1938.

2

It was early morning, just past four. Thick fog covered the grounds and the oak trees whispered through the dark. The wind shook the windows of Gross Breesen house, travelled up through the floorboards and beneath the doors. The sleeping students huddled further into their blankets; the youngest were fearful of ghosts. Only a few students were awake at this time, those unluckily assigned to work in the cowshed. As they dressed in the dark and quietly descended the stairs towards the fields, it felt as if they were the only people in the world who were not sound asleep.

The boys traipsed across the grounds, bleary-eyed and aching from yesterday's toil. Through the fog they could just make out the large shed, white-painted wood against the inky sky. They were armed with shovels and tin buckets. Their stomachs were empty, their hunger fiery, but each boy stifled his yearning for breakfast and furrowed his brow. They reached the shed and paused for a moment to catch their breath. They listened to the soft cattle groans coming from inside. Moments later they were hit by the wall of stench, strongest first thing in the morning. A few boys made noises of disgust as they neared. The shed was an ancient structure; the foundations still stood from its original building in the eighteenth century. The interior stalls were decrepit and rotting; there was no drainage and poor light, making the tasks of mucking it out and milking the cows even more laborious. The students had fixed the shed up with fresh paint and new boards over the years, but it still looked like a relic from another time, as did much of Gross Breesen. The ploughing machinery, the tools and the dilapidated buildings were practically medieval. Every task was completed by hand, without any sort of protection. Any means of relief from the harsh elements, such as wearing gloves, was forbidden. It was Bondy's belief that working with bare hands was an essential part of the students' training.

The Oberschweizer (head milker) was a senior student in his final year of training. His name was Hans,[9] and he was a particularly brutal leader. Utterly infatuated by his own superiority, Hans relished disciplining the dairy trainees. Work in the cowshed was unanimously known as the most difficult on the farm, and the Oberschweizer took it upon himself to scold any student foolish enough to not pull his weight.

'Right, you, Poscho, help me open up,' said Hans, calling Hermann by his Gross Breesen nickname.

Diligently, Hermann pushed down hard on the metal lever and unlatched the huge wooden doors. It took all his strength not to shudder forwards as the smell of festering manure strangled him and the others. He held his breath as he steadied the doors. Inside the shed, 80 Friesians were packed together side by side, and in the far corner was the bull, heavy and magnificent, tipped to win first prize at the local fair had it not been from the 'Jew Farm', as Gross Breesen was known in the surrounding villages.

Next to Hermann was Erich. He had only been at Gross Breesen for a month and was still finding his feet. Next to Hermann, Erich looked rather scrawny; he was a few years younger and had not yet grown coarsened by manual labour like the older boys. Erich was from Memmingen in the south of Germany. His parents lived in a rural village and had scrounged enough money to send their eldest son to North America and Erich to Gross Breesen, in the hope that he could then emigrate with greater ease. There was no prospect of escape from the growing violence for themselves. All efforts went into saving their children. Having barely departed childhood, Erich sorely missed his home and parents, and felt immense guilt for leaving them behind. Erich tried hard to wear a brave face and would only occasionally let on that he was terribly homesick. By the time Erich arrived at Gross Breesen, Hermann was an established member of the community and acted as a mentor, an older brother in whom he could confide. Hermann and Erich became close friends in no time, spurred by living and working in such close quarters and having a shared sense of humour.

'Well, don't just stand there,' barked Hans. 'The shit won't shovel itself!'

The boys scrambled into action. The first task was to clean the shed, shovel out the manure, pile it onto wheelbarrows and take it to the towering dung mound around the back. Hans made sure each student shuddered under the weight of his wheelbarrow in the name of efficiency. Hermann suspected it was also because Hans took pleasure in berating any poor student who collapsed beneath the weight. None of the boys noticed the sun rise. When a few hours passed and the group finally wheeled the last batch of dung to the heap, morning had crept into the corners of the shed and along the animals' flanks. Fresh straw was laid and the shed cleaned till it was spotless. After inspecting every inch, Hans nodded and allowed the feeding to commence.

Hermann helped to load up the wheelbarrows full of sugar beets and hay. Herr Scheier, the Oberinspektor (farm manager and overseer of all agricultural duties), insisted that adding sugar beets to the cattle's diet would speed up milk production. It was also a way to use the surplus beets that took to the farm's soil and grew like weeds. The heavy beets, like small bowling balls, were piled into the wheelbarrows, lugged up the ramps and poured into the troughs. While the cows were distracted by their breakfast, the milking commenced.

Hermann sat atop his three-legged milking stool beneath one of the huge black-and-white speckled animals. He gently stroked the cow's side and reached for her swollen udders. They were all taught the proper technique at the start of the milking term. Hermann pressed and pulled the udders until a spray of warm milk hit the metal bucket in front of him. He continued like this, rhythmically pressing and pulling, until he was certain there was none left, then quickly continued to the next cow. The milkers were as meticulous as machines, and just as hardworking. If there were complaints, they remained unspoken, or were muttered into the steaming buckets, because Hans was always within earshot.

Time passed slowly as the boys grew transfixed by their monotonous task. By midmorning, their backs ached from crouching, their necks were stiff from bowing and their stomachs could no longer be ignored. Outside, the sun was high, a glary silver ball behind thick grey haze. Buckets of fresh milk were lined up at the entrance to the shed, ready to carry back up to the main house. Hans went around to each cow and made sure every drop was extracted. When he was satisfied the job was complete, he excused the boys. While they did not dare complain or admit to their exhaustion, each boy looked as though he could keel over at any moment. They washed their hands and faces in a bucket of clean water near the entrance to the shed.

As they did each morning, the female students traipsed out from the kitchen in the main house carrying large baskets of rye bread with jam, and coffee made from barley. There were significantly fewer girls at Gross Breesen than boys. Many parents thought it inappropriate for their daughters to attend an agricultural school, despite Bondy's insistence that it could mean a ticket out of Germany. Frau Scheier, the farm manager's wife, taught the girls house duties and cooking. At harvest time, the girls helped toil the fields alongside the boys, learned to ride horses and even took lessons in woodworking. Only a few select girls were allowed to train in the cowshed.

Hermann watched as the girls approached with their baskets and pitchers of coffee. The procession stopped short of the shed, placing the morning tea a few yards away, wasting no time getting as far from the boys as possible. Hermann took a pitcher of coffee and poured himself a cup. Only then did he register his aching muscles and the pain that shot up his spine as he stood straight. But he was young, and so such protestations of the body were easy to ignore and dissipated quickly.

Hermann and Erich picked a spot in the closest field and stretched their legs out for the first time all day. Their mouths watered with each bite of bread.

'You know, I don't mind the cowshed,' said Erich through bites of bread. 'Once you get past the smell, of course.'

Hermann chuckled. 'At least we'll be expert milkers by the time we're through.'

Erich was brought up helping his father on farms and was used to the work. It was always his ambition to work on the land. Unlike Hermann, who only knew city life, Erich was perfectly at home lugging hay and caring for animals.

Erich took a big bite of bread. 'I wonder if it will be the same in our new country.'

Hermann pondered this. He tried to imagine a farm in the proposed 'new countries'—North and South America, Canada, Kenya, Australia. But he could not. Hermann sipped his coffee. It was bitter; the coarse granules scraped his tongue. He much preferred the coffee back home.

The boys sat in silence and watched another work group digging for beets in the next field.

'Awful job, that one,' said Erich.

'At least they don't stink like a cow's arse,' Hermann replied.

Erich laughed. The students assigned to the cowshed were avoided by the rest of the farm, as they tended to the cattle twice daily and despite hot showers could never be rid of the smell.

'Have you had any word from back home?' asked Erich.

'My parents are looking for a new flat. They won't tell me why, but I guess my father's work has cancelled their lease. He said it was only a matter of time until they did.'

Neither boy could properly comprehend that their home country wanted them gone. It was an irreconcilable truth that each grappled with, despite years of exclusion and abuse. Both of their fathers were Iron Cross–decorated from their war service. Both fathers, despite their wives' hesitations, refused to leave Germany, repeatedly arguing that their country was far too sophisticated to put up with the Nazis for any stretch of time. Now it was too late; the deterioration of Erich's parents' health, their finances and forced eviction left them no possibility of emigration. The Pollnows faced a similar situation.

Professor Curt Bondy at Gross Breesen, taken by Hermann Pollnow, 1938.

'Sorry to hear,' said Erich.

'They'll be alright. It's just my mother I worry about. Her illness only seems to get worse ...' Hermann sipped his coffee. He squinted and saw Bondy on horseback trotting around the field's perimeter, no doubt inspecting the students' technique and making sure there was no chatter going on during the work shift.

'My mother is ill as well,' said Erich softly. 'And my father. He never quite recovered after the arrest.'

Hermann glanced at Erich and saw tears beginning to well in his eyes.

'Come on,' said Hermann. 'We'd better get back to work. I'd rather not have a run-in with Hans if we're late.'

Erich sniffed and nodded. The two boys joined the rest of their work detail to fix broken panels around the shed before lunch.

*

While Hermann was away at Gross Breesen, Max's worry was unrelenting. The city around them grew more hostile. Friends and neighbours fled; normal life was an old reality. The Pollnows were now settled in the Oberschöneweide neighbourhood, on Schillerpromenade, number 12, and had been there for the past three years. Their old housekeeper, Frau Warnke, had returned home to her family;[10] they had recently employed a new housekeeper, Fräulein Selma, who was the same age as Max.[11] Despite years of service, the AEG was pushing to evict Max and Edith from their Schillerpromenade flat, including the practice rooms AEG leased to Max following his forced resignation. They no longer wanted Jews living in the block.

It was just past 9am. Max was already at the practice and had been for hours; Edith was lying awake in bed, transfixed by the grey light between the heavy drawn curtains. On her bedside table was a picture of Hermann at Gross Breesen in his work outfit—loose-fitting collared shirt, trousers, boots and a cap—mounted on a horse, clasping the reins. He wore a hint of a smile, but Edith could tell he was trying to look more mature than his age, more like a man. Hermann sent her and Max few photos home, and she kept each one in the bedside drawer. This one, though, she framed and looked at each morning as she woke up. Confined to her bed, she followed Hermann in her mind, imagining what he was doing at that moment.

There was a knock at the door. Slowly, it creaked open and Fräulein Selma peered in.

'Good morning, Frau Pollnow. It's a warm day outside.'

Edith smiled faintly. 'Good morning.'

'Would you like some coffee? Some breakfast?'

Edith nodded and Selma disappeared again, returning moments later with a small tin tray holding a silver pot, cup and saucer, and a few slices of bread. Edith was impressed. Already she seemed at home with her tasks.

'Thank you,' said Edith as she attempted to sit up.

Selma was plump with short, brown, curly hair and a maternal air that put Edith immediately at ease. The Pollnows and all other Jews were forbidden to employ a German housekeeper under the age of 45. With careful hands, Selma placed the tray on the bedside table and helped Edith into a seated position. Then she placed a cloth across Edith's chest and cut a small piece of bread.

'There you are,' said Selma, helping the bread into Edith's hand. Edith chewed slowly and motioned for coffee. Her mouth was dry from sleep.

'Thank you,' said Edith.

She took a sip and winced as the hot liquid trickled down her throat.

'I've started lunch for you and Herr Dr Pollnow this afternoon,' Selma said. 'I hope it's to your liking. I used my grandmother's recipe.'

'Thank you,' said Edith. 'That sounds lovely.'

'Would you like to sit out on the balcony? It might be good for you to get some sun.'

Edith paused, deciding whether her body was up to that challenge. 'Perhaps later this afternoon. I'm tired this morning.'

'Of course.'

Max returned for lunch midafternoon. Despite the heat, he wore his suit jacket and only shed it once he was inside the flat. Max was welcomed by the scent of beef and potato stew. He greeted Selma then knocked on the bedroom door softly. If Edith was asleep, he did not want to disturb her.

'Come in.' He heard her voice, high-pitched and airy like a bird. Edith was propped up in bed with the window open, flooding the room with light. In their bedroom was a blond oak-framed double bed and two matching bedside tables, a double-door oak wardrobe, two bedside chairs, a woollen carpet and, above the bed, a crystal chandelier. Out the window and down below was the courtyard, with flowering blossom trees and green hedges.

'Pipchen, how are you feeling today?' he asked gently.

Edith turned to face him. Her hair, now dull and coarse at the ends, was parted in the middle and tucked behind her ears. She still made sure it was tidy every day, though it was a far distance from the days when she would have it styled in elegant waves.

'Tired, always tired,' she replied.

'Why don't we go and sit out on the balcony? It's wonderfully warm. Lunch should be ready soon as well,' said Max, sitting at the end of the bed.

Edith gazed outside again. Two black birds whipped past the window in a flourish. She looked at her husband. His face was marked with worry; his eyes looked sunken and the lines in his forehead grew more pronounced each day.

'Alright,' she said.

Max called for Selma and together they helped Edith into her wheelchair and covered her with a blanket; despite the heat of the day, she still shivered.

'Let's get you out into the sun,' Selma said.

The housekeeper wheeled Edith into the lounge room, unlocked the balcony door and latched both doors to the outside stoppers. Max took the handles of the wheelchair and carefully edged towards the door and, with Selma's help, lifted it over the threshold and onto the balcony landing. It was only a small space, but there was room enough for two chairs, a little wooden table, and potted flowers lining the railing. Edith, pale and thin, relished the afternoon sun. She closed her eyes.

'Thank you, Fräulein Selma,' said Max.

'Of course,' she replied. 'Lunch will be ready soon. When you want to eat, I will serve.'

'Thank you.'

Once Edith was settled, Max went to the bureau, fetched his

typewriter and brought it outside with him. He placed it on the table and threaded a wisp-thin piece of paper, imported from Japan.

'I'm writing to Mutzi. Is there anything you'd like me to say?'

Edith sighed. 'Not really. Just that we're well, not to worry about me. Oh—and that we thoroughly enjoyed his last card! He is a brilliant writer, don't you think?'

'Yes, he writes with great detail.'

'Oh, Max, you had better tell him that we had to sell our shares at the zoo.' Edith sighed, knowing how upset he would be to hear this.

Max nodded.

'Ask him to please write more about what he is getting up to. And that we're always thinking of him ...' Trailing off, she sat in silence while Max typed.

*

4 August 1938

Dear Mutzi,

Your postcard arrived yesterday, but I've only been able to respond to it this evening because of a rush of events.

I'm not sure if you are aware of the latest news concerning us, I'll attach a newspaper article about it. We are facing a completely new situation. It's completely unclear what the future holds, it's not even worth wasting time thinking about it. You can only really plan for the short term. The most pressing issue is the housing situation, which as I predicted is now dire.

We are no longer interested in staying in this suburb; in fact, I think it's unwise for us to stay. For the time being I can't give you more details.

Yesterday was quite horrible: crazy heat you could hardly move in, and in the evening a storm in the West, the likes of which our elders had never experienced ... We didn't get the storm, it only rained a little and didn't cool down much.

Kastan and Wieruscowski were here last night. It was quite nice, even though spirits—mine at least—were and still are low. I'm not sleeping much at night. Mutti doesn't know anything, at least nothing specific. I have to be very careful ...

At the moment, we are on the balcony trying to cool down a bit ...

The three neon fish died on Sunday, one week after we got them. I have no idea why ... At the same time, one of the big mollies also died but that's not such a big loss because we still have so many ...

Weinberg is coming tomorrow evening, to discuss the situation, as he put it. I always look forward to his visits, as the number of decent men I can have an honest discussion with isn't high ...

Mutti just told me to tell you that we sold our shares in the zoo. For now, I don't have anything else to report on.

Stay healthy and keep us in your thoughts.

1000 kisses from Mutti and Vati.

Max reclined in his chair, lifting his face upwards to the sun. Edith mirrored him.

'*Sehr schön,*' he said.

'Lovely,' agreed Edith. Her breaths were shallow.

'Pipchen, are you hungry?' Max asked.

She was not, but Selma had been cooking all day. It would do her good to have at least a small bowl.

Edith and Max made their way slowly to the dining table where two places were set around a silver pot of beef and potato stew with rice. They sat and Selma served them each a portion. Jonny the tomcat meowed at their feet and jumped onto the dining table.

'Get down!' yelled Max. 'Down!'

He shooed the cat from the table and Jonny hissed, retreating for only a few moments before making a second attempt.

'That's it!' said Max. He grabbed the creature, threw him into the hallway and shut the door.

'Don't hurt him, Max! He's only little,' cried Edith.

'What a nuisance he is!' he said, sitting back down.

'He only wants to be near us,' Edith said, eternally sympathetic to her feline companion.

'You mean he wants to be near our meal!'

Edith poked at her stew and took a few small bites before she was overcome by fatigue. She hung her head slightly, and soon went back to bed, leaving Max to finish his meal alone.

The sun remained high and the wind picked up, tousling leaves and dust through alleyways, beyond rooftops. The flowers on the balcony, purple and red and orange, quivered in their pots. Jonny poked at those he could reach on the ledge, jumping up and rubbing his whiskers against them. Max took a cigar from the fresh packet, gifted to him by Edith's mother, Ella, for his birthday, drew it to his lips and held his gasoline lighter to its end, welcoming the familiar warm haze of his exhalation. He watched as Jonny threatened to knock over the flowerpots, before finding a spot between them and nestling himself in the sun.

Max gave the letter to Selma to post and went back to work for the afternoon, where he would stay until very late in the evening.

3

It was after work, in the still, quiet hours of night, that Max's worries descended. The most pressing worry was finding a new flat away from this neighbourhood, because it was no longer safe for the Pollnows to live in Oberschöneweide. Their neighbours grew more hostile, as the Jewish community migrated to pockets of the outer city, or overseas if they were lucky enough to obtain the necessary permits. The feeling of imminent displacement leaked into Max's chest and tightened his throat. *Where would they go? Where could they live in safety?*

Max's mind drifted back to a night a few years ago. He was sitting in the lounge room when through the silence there was a hurried knock on the front door. Max got up and opened it slightly, and when he recognised the man in front of him, he flung the door wide open to let him in. It was their neighbour from the second floor. Nearly a month ago, he had disappeared; no-one knew where he had gone. Concentration camps were known about but never spoken of, and the threat had not yet been so close to home. Max could not forget how his neighbour looked as he stood before him: strikingly thin and grey-skinned, like a shadow.

'Max, I implore you. You must leave immediately. Germany is no longer safe for us, and it will only get worse, mark my words,' he said.

The memory lingered as he took another draw from his cigar. Max had closed the door on his neighbour, thinking he had gone mad. *Leave Germany? And go where?*

They were German, after all. Like so many of his colleagues and friends, Max believed this political unrest would pass, that the German people could not possibly tolerate these Nazi thugs for any real stretch of time. He believed no harm would come to his family given his lifetime of service to Germany.

The neighbour left with his wife and two children for Palestine the next day, and they were never seen or heard from again. These occurrences were not uncommon. And now, Jewish colleagues and friends were doing everything they could, seeking help from anyone with the slightest power to assist in leaving the country. Leaving Germany was not an option for Max and Edith; they did not have the money, for one, and Edith would not survive the upheaval.

By now the night had settled, cool and still, and the streetlamps lit the wide footpath to number 12 Schillerpromenade. The moon gilded the roofs and street signs. While Edith slept, Max had taken to walking in the evenings; never far, only around the nearest block. Now nearing home, he crossed the courtyard garden of their unit block and noticed the sweet, pungent fragrance of the fruit trees on the cusp of their bloom. Although the courtyard was small, there were many trees and flowers, with scents that perfumed the night air. Their smell reminded Max of forests beyond the city, and for a moment he thought of hiking in the Bavarian wilds, skiing in the Alps. So familiar. He breathed in deeply.

He opened the door of the flat and was met with silence before Jonny came bounding towards him, more dog than cat in his boisterous demeanour.

'Get down, you terror,' whispered Max. Jonny whined in objection, clawing at Max's pant leg.

Max was too exhausted to eat. He went to the washroom and splashed his face a few times with icy water. He changed and fell into bed. Hours passed before at last he found a troubled kind of sleep, his mind lured to it by tomorrow's promise, and the small comfort that Mutzi was safe, away from the city; of that much he could be certain.

When I imagine Edith, she is in bed, covers pulled tight up to her chest, looking out a window. Out, perhaps, to the blossoming tree I have seen in a picture of the courtyard at 12 Schillerpromenade. Was it in eyeshot of the Pollnows' bedroom? I cannot know for sure, and yet this is a persistent scene in my imagining of Edith. She might have been a gentle person, sweet and thoughtful and nurturing, who looked out her window each day, unable to walk and confined to her bedroom, imagining for herself another life in which she still had the use of her limbs and a healthy immune system. Perhaps she daydreamed of the past; she was not always bedridden. I imagine that before Edith met Max, her mother, Ella, took her on outings and trips. To the Alps, skiing or springtime walking; to the French coast,

Nice perhaps; and to villages and cities within Germany she had not seen but always wanted to visit. Did Edith like to read? Did she like the theatre? Was she adventurous? If she had not developed a debilitating illness, what might she have done with her days? This picture might not be real, but it is there in my mind, clear as a memory, and I feel it with me. I collect tiny pieces of information, fashion a person from the pictures Harry keeps close to him, and the memories he occasionally shares. The same is true of Max, though I have much more information about him; he authored the letters sent to Harry once he was out of Germany. Max signed the letters from himself and Edith, but the words were always his. Edith's presence in them is felt but in a peripheral way, as if she was in the room, always in Max's consciousness, while he wrote.

Max signed every letter as *Vati* (Dad). His script is assured and strong; it looks to have been written quickly without a second thought. A confident flourish. The only evidence I have of Edith's own script is from a preserved document from our family's collection: an application for an identity card dated 1938.

This trace of Edith is rare and telling. Her script is shaky; I wonder how long it took her to write this signature. Here I have evidence of her hand, of her body in action. To me Edith's writing stands out from the rest of the document, a flicker of the life I am trying to find on an otherwise administrative form. To have this piece of her fills my mind with possibilities. Where was she when she signed it? Most probably she was propped up in bed and Max or Fräulein Selma delivered the document for her to sign. She would have clasped the pen in her hand (left or right?) and written her name slowly, determined.

Antrag auf Ausstellung einer Kennkarte

1. Familienname: Pollnow 1a. ~~Beruf~~:

bei Ehefrauen — geb. Pollack verw. gesch.

bei Namensänderung — früherer Name:

Sondername: [1]

2. Vornamen: Edith
(Rufname unterstreichen)

3. Geboren am: 22. Oktober 1894
(Monatsname ausschreiben)

4. Geburtsort: Glauchau (Sa)
(nötigenfalls Kreis, Regierungsbezirk und, wenn Ausland, Staat)

5. Wohnort: Berlin seit wann? 1902
(Kreis)

6. Wohnung: Berlin Oberschöneweide Schillerpromenade 12
(Straße, Hausnummer)

7. Familienstand: ~~ledig~~ — verheiratet — ~~verwitwet~~ — ~~geschieden~~ *)

8. Bei bestehender Ehe — Eheschließung mit: Dr. Max Pollnow
am 20. Mai 1919 in Berlin

9. Jude [2]: ja — ~~nein~~ *)

10. Staatsangehörigkeit [3] Deutsches Reich: Deutsches Reich

Reisepaß: ausgestellt am 20. Mai 1933 von Polizeiamt Tiergarten *)
(Behörde)

~~Heimatschein?~~ ausgestellt am von *)
(Behörde)

~~Staatsangehörigkeitsausweis?~~ ausgestellt am von *)
(Behörde)

Beruf: ohne Beruf

Ich versichere, daß ich die vorstehenden Angaben nach bestem Wissen und Gewissen gemacht habe.

Als Beweismittel
füge ich bei: Geburtsurkunde — ~~Taufschein~~ — ~~Heimatschein~~ — ~~Staatsangehörigkeitsausweis~~ — ~~Matrikelschein eines deutschen Konsulats~~ — ~~Optionsurkunde~~ *)
habe ich vorgelegt: Reisepaß — ~~Wehrpaß~~ — ~~Anstellungsurkunde~~ (bei Beamten) *)
5 Lichtbilder sind angeschlossen.

(Anzahl der beigefügten Urkunden)

Oberschöneweide, den 19. Okt. 1938

Edith Pollnow geb. Pollack [4]
(Unterschrift — Vor- und Familienname)

*) Nichtzutreffendes streichen.
[1]) Hier ist ein etwaiger Schriftsteller-, Theater-, Künstler- und Artistenname sowie bei katholischen Geistlichen und Ordensangehörigen der in dieser Eigenschaft etwa geführte besondere Name anzugeben.
[2]) § 5 der Ersten Verordnung zum Reichsbürgergesetz vom 14. November 1935 — RGBl. I S. 1333 —.
[3]) Bei mehrfacher Staatsangehörigkeit sind sämtliche Staatsangehörigkeiten anzugeben.
[4]) Stellt der gesetzliche Vertreter des Kennkartenbewerbers den Antrag, so ist der Unterschrift hinzuzufügen: „als gesetzlicher Vertreter des (der) . . . .“

Edith Pollnow's identity card application, 1938.

I put this document back into its plastic sleeve with the others. I think it was Irmgard Veit-Simon, Harry's aunt, who smuggled these papers out of Germany. She was an 'Aryan', not Jewish, and spent the war living in Berlin with the knowledge that all six of her children were either in camps, on the other side of the world, or dead.

I reach to the other side of my desk for the tattered burgundy briefcase—a relic from another world. I found it at my mother's house, in a box. The outside is soft, faded leather and the inside is divided into 12 sections that open up like an accordion. The case is fastened with a gold clasp engraved *Moritz Mädler Leipzig*. From a quick Google search, I learn that Moritz Mädler was a prestigious bag and leather-goods maker in the early 1900s in Germany. Undoubtedly, the briefcase belonged to Max. Or perhaps Max gave it to his son as a gift. I trace the gold clasp with my index finger and wonder if I am also tracing his fingerprints. Inside the briefcase, along with various other documents, is Harry's collection of letters from his parents, which he has kept all these years but long forgotten.

My mother discovered the letters first. She knew I was working on a project about Harry's life and thought they might be of interest to me. When I first laid eyes on them, nearly 100 documents, I was overwhelmed by their weight, transfixed by the pages and pages of words I could not read. Each document was a portal, and I felt the potential of each as I leafed through them—some handwritten, most typed, all marked in some way by old life: a rip, a smudge, a word erased and rewritten, an equation roughly scribbled out, an initial signature practised on the underside of an envelope.

It was a strange experience to come across this collection of papers written by the very people I'd been trying to find. I felt a connection—was it yearning? Yearning to convene with the original authors of these letters who were, and would always be, so far away from me? And yet I could not read the words, line upon line of German, a reminder that these letters were not meant for my eyes. That they ended up here, in front of me, salvaged from an unmarked box in my mother's study in Sydney, was a chance happening that no-one, not least of all the original authors, could have foreseen. I traced the words, trying to find any slight familiarity, but I recognised little more than the name of the addressee: Mutzi.

Since their discovery, I have copied each letter, had it translated, devised a cataloguing system and ordered each chronologically in large ring binders alongside their English counterparts. I've gone through and taken note of every person mentioned in the collection, tabulated each name next to a column: *Traceable? Y/N.* Of course, the central characters are easy to detect: Max, Edith, Ella. Other family members are frequently mentioned: Aunty Irmgard and Uncle Heinz Veit-Simon and cousins Etta (affectionately called Etchen) and Ruth, two of the Veit-Simons' six children. Their visits to Max and Edith are mentioned frequently in the letters. Max wrote to Mutzi about his friends, colleagues, even his patients—people who will only ever be names to me.

I take one of the ring binders down from my shelf and flip to letters dated from mid-1938. Ella wrote to Mutzi on 19 May 1938:

My dearest Mutzilein!

The watch was sent to you today. I hope it's to your taste. Heartfelt thanks for your dear postcard. I am glad to read that you have found the right place and that you are content. Thanks to that detailed letter of yours addressed to your parents, I have already been filled in on everything. It must be lovely for a young person. Your parents were so happy to receive your letter. They are keeping all of your letters safe, so that one day you will be able to read them yourself. Other than that, not much has happened since your departure. At your house it has become much quieter, and Jonny is looking for you everywhere. Your mother is feeling a bit better. The new maid is excellent. Her cooking is brilliant, she is very clean and, most importantly, friendly and diligent. Which is very important for your mother's nerves. I often go out to see her, so that she isn't so lonely in your father's absence. If it is possible, write a card home tomorrow. It's your parents' 20th wedding anniversary. I am writing with great urgency so that you get the letter on time. Next time I'll write more! ...

Loving hugs,
your old Oma.

Oma's words echo in my mind: 'They are keeping all of your letters safe, so that one day you will be able to read them yourself.' What I would give to see the other half of this collection, Hermann's letters to Max, Edith and Ella. I wonder if they still exist somewhere or if, like countless relics, they, too, disappeared beyond the archive, into the realm of forgotten past.

Ella hints that Hermann was happy at Gross Breesen and wrote in earnest to his parents a detailed report of everything he'd been up to. Undoubtedly, he was enthusiastic about his new life as a student of agriculture or, at least, that is what he told his parents. Compared to his alternative, I imagine the enthusiasm was genuine. In Ella's words I feel the peripheral sadness of Hermann's quiet home and his mother's nerves and loneliness. I follow Jonny the cat from room to room searching for his absent master. I picture Edith alone in bed, nothing to do but wonder what happens next. I trace the cracks in the ceiling, the dresser, the closed door. With Edith I am trapped beneath the weight of reality. I know what is ahead; I have seen, we have all seen, but now there is nothing to be done.

I read the letter a couple more times, taking in every detail. Ella's cursive is jagged but controlled; she used a thin black ink pen that still, after all these years, lines the paper with fine clarity. I trace her words with my index finger. What would she think if she could see me, her great-great-granddaughter, forensically examining this card for clues? If Ella stood behind me now, one hand on my shoulder, peering down at my notes, would she point at my inference and say no, I was not like that at all, what I really meant was this? Or perhaps she would tell me to stop poking and prodding, please, leave my words in peace. I don't know, and I won't ever know what these original authors think of me decoding their words, holding them up to the light and then, when I'm finished, resigning them once more to the darkness.

I am fortunate that Harry has never thrown anything away and seems to have a habit of photocopying every important document twice or three times for good measure. His 100 years are all accounted for, especially in the giant collection of photo albums that has been dispersed between his three children. Harry holds a camera in so many of my childhood memories of him: at every family event, every outing, Harry was designated photographer. At family lunches, Harry would sit poised with his camera hanging from his neck. I now know, from discovering his oldest picture collections from the 1930s, that his desire to record and capture life began early, in his teens. I know that while at Gross Breesen he frequently sent pictures home. I know that Edith kept a picture of him by her bedside. I glance up at the pictures of Edith and Max I have stuck on the wall above my computer screen. Max is wearing a white surgeon's jacket with his hair combed back, gazing upwards against a blank background. Edith is sitting at a wooden table outside, skirted by forest, her cane hanging from her chair, staring right at me. I blink. The orange glow of the streetlamp outside colours the white curtain that hangs over my window. I reach up, pull the curtain to one side and unlatch the window. The stiff old frame requires some effort but I get it open and inhale the familiar scent of charcoal chicken from the restaurant across the street. It's quiet out there, pandemic quiet.

I return to researching Gross Breesen. The estate is now a Polish golf and wellness retreat called Pałac Brzeźno. The website documents the history of the Bresna village, which dates back to 1204. It states that the palace and surrounding grounds were constructed as they appear today at the beginning of the nineteenth century. It was renovated in 1913, and despite the war and the Soviets ransacking it at war's end, the palace survived essentially unscathed. Nowhere on the website does it mention its use from 1936 to 1942. Not a word about the students and teachers, the profound significance the farm school had on those lucky enough to attend. I guess this bit of history is only significant to some.

On the website homepage is a rotating carousel of pictures taken around the property. Pristine bedrooms, the dome-shaped original brick cellar, a green mown golf course and the manor house itself from all angles, painted cream with a terracotta roof and old slate-tiled steeple, encircled by manicured hedges. The shape of the building is unmistakable, I recognise it immediately. It looks surreal in colour; I'm used to this place in black and white. In my head I can't help but superimpose the old photos I know so well over these new ones saturated by green and sky blue.

The Gross Breesen Schloss,
taken by Hermann Pollnow, c.1938.

Harry went back there, years ago, when I was much too young to understand the significance. As usual, he took pictures, just as he did in 1938. In my mind, Gross Breesen is a sanctuary, its walls embedded with history and hope. I can see the school's influence on Harry if I think about it. The most obvious is the inextricability of work and self. This also came from his father, I think. But hard work, in whatever form, was at the core of Harry's being until he retired (at age 92). There was no alternative to hard work, no excuse for mediocrity. Now I realise that this view was formed in the years when, for Harry, hard work was the difference between life and death.

In the eighteenth century, Gross Breesen was owned by nobility. Their descendants were the Polish-Jewish Rohr family who, in 1936, leased the estate rent-free to the Reichsvertretung der Deutschen Juden, an umbrella organisation representing Jewish interests, so that a group of young German Jews could be trained in agriculture. There were more than 100 students at the Gross Breesen training farm, from all over Germany, aged between 15 and 25. They were taught all the subjects they'd begun to learn prior to expulsion from school, as well as farm, wood and metalwork—skills these mostly middle-class adolescents from the big cities probably never imagined they would master. Their hands coarsened and bonds of camaraderie deepened. This was no coincidence, as Bondy oversaw the rigorous administration process and only allowed in those whose character would fit the build of the school. Strong character was more important to Bondy than physical fitness or intellect. The students were taught to work for the greater good of the collective and to hold themselves to the highest possible moral code. In return, the students were granted a semblance of freedom, despite the rigid structure of each day. Away from the cities and with no exposure to the worsening political situation, Gross Breesen was a small oasis; the outside world was not visible beyond the trees.

Harry met his lifelong best friend, Eric, formerly Erich, at Gross Breesen. I have memories of visiting Eric and his wife, Ruth, along with Eric's daughter, Diana, and son, Peter, who are close friends of Mum's. I remember Saturdays spent at Harry and Lynn's house in Lindfield, in Sydney's north: rows of thick sausages sizzling on the barbecue, Harry and Eric sitting side by side in full sun, their olive-skinned torsos baking, each holding a VB stubby. The only time Harry ever spoke German was to Eric. I remember going to Eric's funeral when I was a teenager. It was the first funeral I ever attended. At the time, I didn't fully understand how profound this loss was for Harry. Eric was the only person close to him who came from the same place, shared the same mother tongue, the same grief. Eric was at Gross Breesen with Harry when the outside world finally forced entry and stole away with their freedom. The spell was broken in the early hours of 9/10 November 1938.

We arrive at Harry and Lynn's Kiama unit at midday on the dot. The unit is in a recently built block, all white and glass exteriors and overlooking the freshly mown rugby field. Beyond it, the ocean. We press the buzzer. I can picture Lynn getting up and walking to the intercom. We hear her voice: 'Hi, Julia. Hi, Tess.' The heavy glass door clicks open, and I push it forward. We step into the silver lift and ascend smoothly. The lift speaks: 'Level three'. We turn right and walk to the white front door; our steps echo on the beige tiles. Mum carries a green bag; inside it are two large tubs of Lynn's favourite baba ganoush from the

Persian grocer on the Willoughby high street. I knock on the door three times and listen for the movement behind it. Footsteps shuffling and Lynn's voice. 'That will be Julia and Tess, dear.' The door opens.

'Welcome, welcome,' says Lynn, and I give her a big hug. I've missed her.

'Good to see you, Lynn,' I say and walk inside.

'Hi, Lynn,' says Mum. 'You're looking well. Been for a swim this morning?'

'You bet! It's finally warming up a bit.'

Lynn swims every day, sometimes twice, down at the Kiama rockpool.

The flat is small but bright and neat: open kitchen, lounge room and adjoining balcony, partitioned with glass sliding doors. Harry is sitting in his armchair in the living area, facing out to the view. I wave to him and smile, and he returns the gesture. His soft white hair is combed back neatly, and he wears a navy-blue tracksuit jacket over his knees, beige socks underneath orthopaedic sandals, a pale blue-and-brown checked short-sleeved shirt and thick black reading glasses fastened with a black string around his neck. Next to Harry is a glass of fluoro-green Staminade, today's newspaper, a small brown leather picture album, and his copy of *The Last Veit-Simons from Berlin: Holocaust, Gender, and the End of the German-Jewish Bourgeoisie*, a book written by two historians about his Uncle Heinz and Aunty Irmgard Veit-Simon and their six children. According to the book's authors, the Veit-Simon family was a perfect case study for the demise of Berlin's Jewish elite. Harry's copy is dog-eared and creased from his daily interrogations. The picture of Heinz and

Irmgard on the front cover of the book is the same picture that is framed on the television stand, next to the pictures of Max and Edith. In the pictures, separate but joined by the bi-fold frame's spinal hinges, Max is in his white surgeon's coat over a suit and tie, posing seated on a diagonal angle. This reveals a facial profile almost identical to Harry's. He looks upwards, and while he is not outwardly smiling, there is warmth in his face. Edith, on the other side of the frame, is pictured sitting in a long, dark-coloured skirt and coat, her curled hair framing her face beneath a woollen cap. She sits in an armchair in what looks like a lion's enclosure at the Berlin Zoo, clutching a lion cub under each arm, with an expression of calm that seems out of place given the scene of the picture. Above Harry's armchair hangs an illustration of the SS *Strathallan*, the P&O passenger cruiser that brought him to Australia in July 1939, with an inset picture of Harry and Eric smiling, looking much older than teenagers.

'Hiya, Harry,' I say, leaning down and hugging him, pressing my cheek into his. His thick hands, quivering, clasp mine.

'Hello!' he says, and smiles.

'You remember me? I'm Tess, your granddaughter.'

He nods. I take a seat on the cushioned armchair opposite his.

'It's turning into a beautiful day,' I say.

'Yes. *Keine Wolken, blauer Himmel.*'

'What does that mean?'

He lifts his right arm up and slowly motions across the horizon.

'No clouds, blue sky.'

I follow his gaze, beyond the neighbour's yard, beyond the

green rugby field skirted by white pickets, beyond the tips of the spindly Norfolk pines, up to the sky. Charlie the cat sleeps under the heavy wooden table, his thicket of fur stretched out over the cool tiles. Two magpies are perched on the next-door neighbour's fence, scratching their grey talons on the weather-worn timber.

'So, are you well?' Harry asks me.

'Yes, thank you. I'm still studying. You know, I was planning to go to Berlin this year.'

'Oh, yeah? Why would you want to do that?'

'I want to go back to where you lived when you were young. With your parents.'

He contemplates this. 'Berlin … Berlin is alright. Just a big city. I haven't been there in a long time.'

'I'm writing a lot about your life, Harry. I'm very interested in your history.'

'Yes, well. There's not much to say about it, really.'

Each time I see Harry, I tell him that I am gathering information about his life and the family's history. He asks me why, and I tell him that I am writing to preserve a part of his story. His reaction is usually the same: he says he's happy to share with me what he can remember, but I don't think he understands why I am so interested. Perhaps it is a symptom of my generation, a conditioning, to be captivated by people who have witnessed the historical events we constantly see portrayed on our screens and newsfeeds. To Harry it is his life, unextraordinary, marked by light and dark, as all lives are. And the part that I'm interested in, the very beginning, happened so long ago. It is buried beneath 100 years of other experiences, memories, emotions. It is the distance between this old life and the present that is enthralling to me, yet tricky for Harry. There is much that his mind will not allow him to access, despite his best efforts.

But there is also much that he remembers in vivid detail, and if I'm lucky I'll see a quick flash of the young man I'm trying to find. I often wonder if I am asking too many questions or, worse, forcing my own projections onto the man who has so generously shared everything he can with me. Sometimes I feel as if I am an intruder wandering through a space in which I don't belong, that isn't meant for me. And for what, to what end? I am free to wander back out the same way I entered, unburdened by the weight of direct memory. For Harry there is no such exit.

There's not much to say about it, really.

'We went back there, years ago. To Berlin,' says Lynn from the kitchen. 'Harry, do you remember when we went back to Berlin?'

'Yes.'

'This was back in the 1970s,' says Lynn. 'I remember we went into a shop and the man said, "Where do you come from?" I pointed to Harry and said, "*Er ist Berliner!*" The man looked at us like we were idiots. He didn't believe Harry was from Berlin because he wouldn't speak a word of German, not for the whole trip! I had to speak for us.'

'How did you feel when you went back?' I ask Harry.

He shrugs. 'I didn't have any particular feelings about it.'

'You must be disappointed that you can't go to Berlin anymore,' Lynn says to me, as she walks out to the balcony and places a plate of ham, sliced tomato, lettuce and cheese on the wooden table.

'Yes and no. I wouldn't want to be there now, with everything that's going on.'

'Too right. Best to stay put until this craziness is over.'

'It could be a lot worse,' says Mum. 'We're not at war.'

Harry picks up the small, brown photo album next to him and begins to flick through it. The pictures are from another time: smaller than palm size, sepia, mostly snapshots of Harry's adolescent life in Germany. Streetscapes, iconic monuments, bustling intersections at Alexanderplatz and Unter den Linden. The animated Kurfürstendamm esplanade, hundreds of citizens crossing footpaths and sitting at street-side restaurants. Train stations decorated with the Olympic rings of 1936. The pictures are vibrant fragments of metropolitan life, turned sinister by the banners and flags branded with swastikas in nearly all of them.

'Where is this place?' Harry asks, looking up from the album at us and around the room. How different these two worlds must appear, this one here around us and the other in the palm of his hand.

'We're in Kiama. This is our retirement unit. We've lived here for over two years now,' Lynn tells him patiently, as if for the first time.

'Have we?' He raises his eyebrows, looks at me and shrugs. 'My memory is very bad.'

'It's alright, Dad,' says Mum. 'You remember who we are?'

'Yes.'

'That's the most important thing. Lynn's here. Charlie's here. You're living in paradise.' She motions out to the view.

'Yes, it's a nice place,' says Harry.

'And your memory is not that bad,' says Mum. 'Your long-term memory is actually very good.'

'Yes, I remember some things well.'

It astounds me how Harry can remember certain details, scenes, from his life as far back as his early childhood. For instance, he remembers when he was small and stuffed any unwanted dinners into his wooden rocking horse. Max eventually found the source of the rancid stench and disciplined his son accordingly. Harry remembers the route he took to walk to school and through the Tiergarten; he can describe the layout of Bahnhof Zoo in detail and list the order of stations on his old train line. He remembers these daily movements and commutes through his old city as if they're embedded in his muscles. Close as yesterday.

'Now, a certain letter arrived yesterday for someone.' Lynn nods in Harry's direction. 'I was waiting for family to be here to open it. What do you reckon? Should we open it before or after lunch?' We're sitting out on the balcony, our chairs angled towards Harry.

'Let's do it before lunch,' says Mum. 'Tess, go and get the letter. It's over on the desk near the computer.'

I return from inside with a thick, A4-sized envelope. It has the Government of New South Wales insignia in the corner and bears an air of importance. I am certain this is the one Mum was talking about. It's heavy; there must be more than one letter in here. The recipient line reads: *Dr Harry Peters*. I hand him the envelope and sit down.

'For me?' he asks us.

'Yes! For you,' Mum replies. Slowly, Harry prises the large envelope open, and three smaller ones fall into his lap. He picks up the largest of the three and carefully slides his thumb across the seal. Inside is a card; its exterior is matte gold with a floral pattern across the front. We hold our breath. I watch his eyes trace the card.

'Who's it from, Dad?' asks Mum.

'Read it out loud, Harry!' I say.

'Dear Dr Peters,' he begins. He reads slowly and glances up at us, pausing for theatrical effect.

'I am pleased to hear that you celebrated your 100th birthday. My sincere congratulations and best wishes on this very special day. Queen Elizabeth.'

'Well, that's very nice, isn't it,' says Lynn.

Harry re-reads the letters and looks up. 'They say I am 100!' He falls quiet, perhaps wondering how this could possibly be true.

'You are 100, dear.'

'Am I?' he looks at me then rolls his eyes.

'Look, it's signed,' says Mum.

'Surely that's not her real signature, Mum.'

'You never know. How many people in the Commonwealth turn 100 every year? Not many, I'll bet.'

'How many people are turning 100?' asks Harry.

'I don't think a lot of people turn 100, Dad.'

'Harry, I have never met anyone who was 100 except you. Not in my whole life,' says Lynn.

'No?'

'Never. It's not very common.'

Harry looks inquisitively at Lynn. 'Did I turn 100?'

Mum, Lynn and I laugh.

'Yes, dear. Three weeks ago.'

'On the ninth of August,' says Mum.

Harry frowns.

'You turned 100 on the ninth of August. That's why you got the letter from the Queen.'

'Where is this letter from the Queen?'

Mum hands the letter back to Harry and he reads it again.

'An endless conversation, they call this,' says Lynn.

I watch as Harry pores over his letters: the one from the Queen again, and the others from the Prime Minister, the Governor-General and the New South Wales Premier, all congratulating him on being alive for 100 years. It's hard to comprehend how much time 100 years really is—how much happens, changes, disappears. In 1920 it must have seemed like the dawn of a new world; in 2020 it feels the same.

'About time for lunch, I think,' says Lynn.

Mum and I grab a plate and make a sandwich each, then Mum grabs another and makes one for Harry.

'Thank you!' he says as she hands him the plate.

These days, conversations with Harry often get on a loop, as if his brain thinks in a circular rather than linear motion. He gets fixated on a topic, one he can remember clearly, such as the Berlin suburb he grew up in, or the route he used to take to visit his cousins, the Veit-Simons, at their villa in Dahlem. I understand this: it must feel comfortable, normal, to latch onto old, engrained knowledge when so much short-term memory is unfamiliar. I jot down every detail to write up later.

'You take the Stadtbahn and get out at Thielplatz. Then you walk up to the Gelfertstrasse, go along for a while, till you reach Meisenstrasse. It's the place on the left.'

'That's how you got to the Veit-Simons' house?'

'Yes.'

'Did you travel there with anyone?'

'No, I went on the train alone.'

He repeats the route a handful of times, each time like it's the first.

When we've finished our sandwiches, I lean towards him and ask, 'So, Harry, what would you say is the secret to living a long life?'

'Beg your pardon?' says Harry, leaning his hearing aid towards me.

'What is the secret to living to 100?' I ask again.

'Well … that's an interesting question, isn't it. I think … I think it's difficult because a lot of the time your health does not depend on you.' I nod and wonder if he is referring to his mother.

'Very true,' says Lynn. 'My observation is that you've always been very moderate. You've never drunk alcohol to excess, always kept fit.'

'Stayed at work until you were 92,' says Mum.

'Yes, I've always been quite fit,' says Harry. 'Especially when I was young.'

'We all were when we were young,' says Lynn.

'That was a very long time ago,' says Harry.

I do not receive a definitive answer from Harry, probably because there isn't one. Either you live to see 100, or you don't. People survive incredible situations and live well into old age, and others practise moderation, suffer no hardship and die young. I have become preoccupied by death's timing lately, and how each of us really has such a short time on earth. How being born in a certain country at a certain time can have such a monumental impact on the trajectory of your life. I had the miraculous fortune of being born in Australia without the slightest threat of persecution. Harry was a refugee; he came here stateless, fleeing mortal persecution with nothing to his name but the required 50 pounds of landing capital, lent to him by the Australian Jewish Welfare Society. Today, people with even less come here seeking asylum and are treated as criminals, because they had the misfortune of being born in one country and not another.

The plates are cleared and we each nurse a cup of tea. Harry returns to his photo album. He studies the pictures meticulously, lingers on each one as if each is unlocking old, familiar knowledge. Lynn tells me I'm free to take some of Harry's pictures home to scan but only a few at a time.

'He likes to look at them before he goes to sleep and would get very upset if he couldn't find them,' she says.

We move inside, and very soon Harry nods off. The standing lamp above him illuminates the right-hand side of his face, the two deep furrows on his brow and the thin lines that run from his nose to the corners of his mouth. I take a handful of pictures from Harry's album: one of the Pollnows' courtyard garden, one of Bahnhof Zoo, and a few others: nondescript streets, trees, a tangle of bicycles on a street corner.

In the doorway we say our farewells. I look over Lynn's shoulder and see that Harry is still dozing, with his tracksuit jacket draped over his knees like a blanket.

Unter den Linden, taken by Hermann Pollnow, c.1936.

View from Tiergarten, taken by Hermann Pollnow, c.1936.

4

7 August 1938

Dear Mutzi,

For your 18th birthday, your Mutti and I send you our best wishes. Above all, we hope that you remain healthy. Hopefully you can bring your apprenticeship in Gross Breesen to a successful end and then dedicate yourself to the profession you've chosen, as a man with experience. If you should then find yourself in a foreign country, you will always know that back home you have parents who love you forever and whose best wishes will always be with you. Maybe there will come a time when we will meet again, and you can let us live with you on your farm. It'll be a fair amount of time though, and we'll just have to see how we can get through this. Now, the sky is full of black clouds and I am not sure what the future entails for all of us. The apartment question has become our number one priority, and I'm doing everything I can to find a way to carry on. Mutti's health makes things considerably more difficult. We will see.

We hope that by the time that this letter arrives, you will already have the suitcase in your possession. You can finally open it now, but it won't contain many big surprises ...

Hopefully the cake is to your liking. Fräulein Selma also wishes you happy birthday. Lollies, chocolate and the sabbath shirt are all from Oma. The pralines from Lindt are from Mutti. I did not include any cigarettes. Take a picture in your Sunday best but let it be a good one! Please send the suitcase back to Oma (Kaiser Allee 31a). Send the keys separately in a letter. We hope that your birthday party is merry and enjoyable. I assume you will let us know. Once again, our best wishes for your new year of life and all that follow.

Best wishes and a thousand kisses from Mutti and Vati.

8 August 1938

My dear Mutzilein,

One, two, three—time flies and we fly with it. Eighteen years ago, your father handed a small squeaking baby to me. You lay there in my arms as he watched beaming with joy. Now you are a big strong man, who will soon venture out into the world. Let me embrace you for this important day, your birthday. I wish you all the best. Especially, good health and happiness in your profession, which I'm sure will bring you much joy. I fulfilled your wishes as best as I could and hope you are happy with your present. Hopefully everything arrives intact. Let the wine, Schillerlocken [smoked fish]*, sausages and cigarettes please your tastebuds and make sure to have fun. You only celebrate your 18th once.*

A warm embrace,
your old Oma.

Hermann tucked the letters from his parents and Oma back into his bedside drawer, took off his dirty work clothes and walked briskly to the showers. There was only a short time between the work shift and commencing the evening activities. Hermann put on a clean shirt and trousers and made his way to the music hall, where Bondy would give a short lecture before dinner. He was met in the corridor by his bunk mates and Erich, who patted him on the back as they walked.

'Happy birthday, Poscho,' said Erich.

'Thank you.' Hermann smiled in reply, pleased his friend remembered. While his family had sent him thoughtful gifts, it was not the same as being home. It was the first birthday he had spent away from Berlin and his parents.

'Eighteen! How does it feel?' asked young Erich.

Hermann chuckled. 'No different, really.'

The students sat in the music hall and waited for Bondy to stand and commence the evening.

'Quiet, please,' Bondy said.

The room fell silent immediately.

'I hope everyone had a good day today. One of you in particular.'

Hermann's heart raced.

'Please join me in wishing a very happy birthday to our Herr Pollnow.' Bondy clapped and the room cheered.

'Happy birthday, Poscho!' they cried. Hermann grinned and looked around the room. A few hands patted his back and those next to him shook his hand vigorously.

'Eighteen is a milestone for everyone. You're a man now, with new responsibilities. I'm happy you get to celebrate here at Gross Breesen with your fellows,' said Bondy.

'Alright, let's continue. This evening, Jens will read from his favourite poet, Wolfskehl, a poem you can later discuss among yourselves. It's called "And Yet We Are Here". Thank you, Jens, please come up here and begin.'

Always driven, always in the bite of the blast—
Was the burden of life ever bitterer on earth?
Has harsher yoke pressed on calloused shoulders,
The plough of dark destiny cut deeper furrows?
Were death and dread ever quite so near?
And yet we are here!

And yet we lifted our foreheads over and over,
And yet our songs of thanks, our prayers and paeans mounted,
When air and light stole through a rift of the mouldy dungeon,
They found us bowed on the book, at God's work, the workers!
Our hearts did not break though our lot was austere,
And yet we are here!

Terrible Fate, you bring weeping and lust to kill,
All day you crouch in corners, threaten and leer,
All night you gnash your teeth and lurk by our pallet.
When we sobbed, swore, implored, it was you who spoke.
Only Hatred replied with savage jeer.
And yet we are here!

Yes, yet we are here, and must remain,
Sucking at pain as at honeycombs.
The others go—are allowed to! Our hour
Once shall know why He suffered our tears.
Then when the trumpet's holy Yes rings clear,
We shall be here![12]

Jens gave a small nod at the poem's close and took a seat.

'Thank you, Jens, and what a wonderful poet is our Karl Wolfskehl. I encourage you all to read him and perhaps speak to Jens, who clearly has an interest in his works,' said Bondy.

'I will not keep you for much longer, as I know that you are all keenly awaiting your dinner. Tonight, we return to the concept of awareness, awareness of ourselves, Bewusstmachung. As you all well know, it is my duty to educate and prepare you for life beyond this farm, wherever that might be. You have been told that your Jewish faith, however strong your beliefs, is something to be thwarted, extinguished. You must reject this, hold steadfast against it and any other teaching that devalues us as people. You must invite self-awareness, self-assuredness, because it is this knowing of oneself that strengthens the character and the spirit.'

The room was silent.

'You must all look inwards. Become aware of your shortcomings, your fears, your prejudices.'

Silence.

'You must not allow yourself to be defeated by them. Instead, you must confront them and master them! Ask yourselves this: do I live according to the ethics and standards set out for me?'

A few students nodded.

'The stronger our bonds with one another are, and the stronger our connection with our traditions and ideology, the stronger we become as individuals, with a much greater likelihood of success in the next phase of life. With Bewusstmachung, self-awareness, we throw light on our own fears, uncertainties and guilt, and correct the distortions of reality to which we are constantly exposed. With self-awareness, we may live with a higher degree of self-criticism and self-control.

'So I ask you, as you go about your days here, to practise this self-awareness. Think hard about your choices, about what you do each day and why you do it. Lebenskunde is this consciousness. Above all, you must be honest with yourself and with others.'

There was silence for a moment, then Bondy lifted his arm to motion the group into chorus, as he did at the end of each session.

To thine own self be true
And it must follow as the night the day.
Thou can'st not then be false to any man.[13]

To the younger students, these talks made little sense. Bondy's sweeping oratory and philosophising flew over the heads of many in the group, but the reverence and certainty with which he spoke told those students that his words were important. To Hermann and the older students, these talks were always interesting, even if at times their relevance was not immediately apparent. Bondy's lectures about ethics and self-awareness were a regular occurrence, an important antidote to the degradation of self the students had grown used to in the outside world.[14]

After a meal of chicken soup, Hermann shared the cake sent from his parents with the rest of the students. With full bellies and heavy limbs, they soon retired to their beds. A troubled sleep descended on Hermann slowly as the day's work blanketed him in exhaustion. He dreamed that he was a small child sitting on the floor of his old bedroom. The door opened to his mother and father reading in the living room, Max on his armchair and Edith on the lounge. The room was bright and serene. Max looked up from his book and beckoned Hermann over to him but Hermann was trapped, surrounded by the tracks of his model train set. The train circled him, faster and faster, and suddenly Hermann was in a train himself, shooting through a city, a city that was Berlin but somehow unrecognisable, as if there had been a shift in the night and the streets were suddenly foreign.

I watch as he ponders my last question, his brow furrowed, staring at a point just down from my right shoulder. He's tired today. Lynn and Mum are outside talking. Harry and I sit beside each other on the armchairs facing the television. Max and Edith are here too, framed on the television stand.

'Harry, tell me more about Gross Breesen.'

'It was a big place for farming. We worked fairly hard. Nothing out of the ordinary, really. We had horses and cows, we had to clean the cows, look after the horses, ploughing and other farm work.'

'Do you remember Professor Bondy?'

'Yes, vaguely. He was the leader of that school ...'

'Gross Breesen.'

'Yes, Gross Breesen.'

'Can you tell me about him? What was he like?'

'He was a good man, but very strict.'

'Do you remember his lectures?'

'No, not really. I remember ... I remember he used to give talks, but I'm not sure what about.'

I search his face for any flicker of recollection. I would love to have his memory to work from, to be able to confidently see Harry as Hermann, one of the teens who sat and listened to Bondy speak in the evenings at Gross Breesen. In the narrative timeline of Harry's early life, Gross Breesen and his imprisonment in Buchenwald Concentration Camp sit side by side. Their association is close; both places were far from home, surrounded by tall forests. Both were departures of a sort. A departure from familiarity, from adolescence and life as he knew it.

'Harry, do you remember Kristallnacht?

'Kristallnacht?'

'Yes, do you remember when you were arrested? You were at Gross Breesen. Do you remember anything about it?'

'Well ... I remember they came, the Nazis, and took us away. I don't know when that was.'

'It was in 1938.'

'Yes, well. We were transported to a concentration camp. That wasn't terribly nice.'

'How did you feel when that happened?'

'Well … depressed. There was no physical … they didn't bash us up or anything like that.'

I nod and let him think.

'I went to Buchenwald, that was the concentration camp. That wasn't a very … not a holiday place. Although one fellow did say that, and he was arrested in the camp for saying that. It was an unpleasant place. But they didn't bash us up or anything like that. In fact, I can't remember what we did there all day.'

'Did you feel frightened when you were in there?'

'No. I don't know how long I was there.'

'Do you remember anything else about the camp?'

'Not really. It was a long time ago, you know. I can't really tell you what we did all bloody day.'

These memories are delicate, and I am careful where I tread. As we both fall quiet, I wonder what it is I am searching for with these questions. To get a sense of how Harry was feeling during this time, I suppose, though it's not hard to imagine that any 18-year-old would be terrified being arrested and sent to Buchenwald. I decide that's enough; there's no use searching for new information where there isn't any. I divert our conversation to something lighter, as I can see he's off somewhere else, staring into nothing.

'Harry, do you remember skiing at Charlotte Pass? Do you remember the snow?'

'Yes.'

I retrieve one of the tomes from under the television stand containing hundreds of pictures of race weeks down at the snow.

This particular batch looks to have been taken in the mid-1980s.

'There you are.' I point to a man wearing big square sunglasses and a beanie, a race number pinned to his jumper, poles up mid-stride on cross-country skis, the great white mounds of the Kosciuszko main range in the distance.

'Yes, that's me.'

Later, back home, I return to the letters. I find the pages written by Max in the months leading up to Kristallnacht. At that time, the most pressing matter for the Pollnows was that the AEG evicted them from the flat at Schillerpromenade and Max spent every spare moment searching for a new place to live. As well as this, the law was changed to restrict the work of Jewish medical practitioners, stating that Jewish doctors could only treat Jewish patients. For ease of recognition, all Jews were to change or add their middle names to the uniform Israel for men and Sara for women.

On 29 August 1938, Max wrote to Hermann:

Dear Mutzi,

... The situation has changed. On Saturday I received a letter from the medical board advising that I am [only] *allowed to treat Jews. This is great news especially because of Mutti. I doubt much else will come of this.*

After I received this letter, I went to the AEG to try to negotiate a retraction of the eviction. The person in charge could not give a concrete answer, but I think we'll get a postponement of the date. This would be a great help, it seems almost impossible to me to find an apartment by

1 October. There's no point staying here, the Jewish population in Oberschöneweide and surrounds is thin on the ground, and they all want to leave anyway …

They all want to go but somehow, they are all still here. The people who are currently handing in affidavits for the USA have to wait until March to speak to the consulate. It is all so uncertain, and as far as I'm concerned we have to wait until September, which will surely hold some surprises for us …

The clinic is becoming quieter and quieter, but it's not quite dead yet. If it's so cold, I could send you my small fur coat, or will you be able to hold out until you visit in December? …

Have you heard about the 'first name' question? I have already pondered over this for you. Before the month of October, you can still change your non-Jewish [middle] *name into a Jewish first name that's in their list. That way, you won't need to be given the generic name of 'Israel' as your first name. 'Lupu' is one of the names on the list and it also sounds the most like Ludwig. So that would then make you 'Hermann Lupu Pollnow'. I don't think that is such a bad idea, as at least the two first letters of your Opa will remain. What do you think? …*

I will gift your klepper boat and toy train tracks to Sabottke the day after tomorrow and assume you don't have a problem with that. Now, I've written enough. We are going to have dinner now and Fräulein Selma can bring the letter downstairs.

Stay safe and, as always, many kisses from Mutti and Vati.

Max was surrounded by friends and colleagues who, as the

second half of 1938 pushed on, saw that it was unwise to stay in certain neighbourhoods and sought housing in different, safer suburbs, or even abroad. The competition for housing at this time must have been fierce; on top of all the other stresses, this would have taken an immense toll on Max, physically and mentally. As the sole income earner for the Pollnows, and Edith's primary carer, life weighed heavily on him.

Eight days later, on 6 September 1938, he wrote:

> *Right now, it looks like we will have to move out on the first of October, despite not actually having a new apartment to move into. I've no idea how we will sort this mess out. There is almost nothing left we can do. Oma was here not long ago and showed us your postcard. There's a problem with the name issue that I wrote to you about: they can demand a fee of between 5 and 500 RM. Since you can't be sure how much it costs in advance, we have decided not to change our names.*

It was during this week of September that Max, after much painful scouring, finally secured a new flat for the Pollnows, on Johannisstrasse in North Berlin. On 13 September, Max wrote this letter to Hermann:

> *Dear Mutzi,*
>
> *Your letter arrived yesterday. We were very happy to have received it since we haven't heard from you in a while. We're glad to know that you're doing well. The photos are very nice, particularly the one where your hand is in your pockets.*

Oma, who was here today, is very jealous. She is going to have a browse in the store on the Martin Lutherstrasse. Do you want anything in particular? Coat, pants or a jacket maybe? Difficult to buy this sort of thing without having tried them on first.

As for us, I have the following to report: after a lot of effort, I have found an apartment that suits us near the Oranienburgerstrasse in North Berlin. However, the contract has not been finalised yet. I hope that gets done soon. The apartment is in terrible condition and must be renovated from the ground up. That will take many weeks. So, I've asked the AEG to allow us to stay here until the end of October and really hope they'll go for it. It's all very tedious and nothing is really going smoothly. You have to use all your energy just to keep your nerves intact and try to get control of what is really a difficult situation. Oma helps as much as she can, which is really important, as I'm trying to make sure that Mutti is never alone. We obviously have to downsize and so the dining-room furniture, which is mostly unnecessary nowadays anyway, must go. This, of course, won't be easy.

Otherwise, I have nothing interesting to tell you. Mutti is currently having a nap on your couch, which Selma and I moved to the salon where the grand piano used to be. At least, like this, Mutti can lie down comfortably and doesn't have to curl up, like she would on the smaller couch.

So, my dear boy, stay safe, have a good time and, if at all possible, write again soon.

A thousand wishes and kisses from Mutti and Vati.

I imagine Max writing these words and see a man on the brink of collapse, out of hope. Finally, he had found somewhere to live, but the flat was completely dilapidated and required significant renovations before they could even begin to move in. I look for other clues about their social life; they would no longer have a dining room, but there was little need for one, anyway. The Pollnows would not have entertained like they used to; they rarely had visitors anymore, except for close friends and family. They sold the grand piano, once a cherished part of their home. I imagine that, to avoid worrying Edith and causing her more distress than she already felt, Max would have kept his apprehension to himself, perhaps revealing his distress to Hermann alone in these letters. It is impossible to imagine exactly how Max felt during these months. I can only speculate, yet his written words show traces of his emotions and fears, inflections of what life was like for the Pollnows as the country around them fell further into chaos.

On 4 October, Max wrote to Hermann:

Dear Mutzi,

Your postcard's just arrived, thank you ... Uncle Heinz and Aunty Irmgard were here recently. They were away (in Kudowa and Duhnen) and have recovered somewhat. Rolf is going back to the Netherlands ... Ruth is also heading out soon.[15] *Tomorrow (5 October) is Oma's birthday. She is coming over in the afternoon. Call us tomorrow at 6 (reverse charges) if you haven't written to her. Hopefully this postcard will reach you in time. There's not much to say about the new apartment.*
The tradesmen are in but are working really slowly. We aren't

sure when we can move in. There's nothing to do here. The few people I'm actually allowed to treat seem to be in good condition. And there are fewer and fewer patients because so many are emigrating.

Loebmann has gone. Even blind Michel and his wife left. Jäger is doing fine, but he's still in the clinic.[16] *Fourteen days ago, I operated on him.*

Mutti's condition hasn't changed and she's not well.

Sending you our greetings and kisses, Your Vati.

And on 22 October, Edith's birthday, Max wrote:

Dear Mutzi,

Thank you for your letters. We were very happy to receive them.

The birthday letter arrived early this morning and Mutti was very happy about it ...

We are sending you some cake that Selma baked today (the pipe is too nice to be kept in your pocket).

I am writing to you right after our phone call. Mutti was really pleased with it. I would have loved to have spoken with Bondy but seeing that he was very busy, I understand that it wasn't possible.

Etchen[17] *just called and told us she was very happy to receive your letter. She sent a letter to Chamberlain after the Munich Conference.*[18] *Today she received a reply, with Chamberlain's signature.*

Right now, it's Sunday evening. I've slept well and had

coffee. This morning, I was in the city, visiting an acquaintance of Jäger, who wants to be operated on for a hernia. Now I want to finish your package, in order to send it tomorrow. After that, I will write a letter to the buyer of our dining-room furniture because he sent me a bad cheque ...

Stay safe and write back to us soon.

Many greetings and kisses from Mutti and Vati.

This was the last letter Hermann received from his father before Kristallnacht, the Night of Broken Glass.

In the early hours of 10 November, Hermann was in the cowshed. The first few hours of the dairy shift unfolded as they did every morning. The boys swept out the rancid insides of the barn, replaced the hay and laid out the feed. While they did not usually speak during their shift, the silence between the boys this morning was different, tense. A few days ago, news reached the farm that Polish-Jewish teen Herschel Grynszpan shot the German diplomat Ernst vom Rath in Paris. Grynszpan was 17, only a year younger than Hermann. Quiet talk and speculation spread through the farm about what was to transpire. Some students applauded Grynszpan's heroism; others, while sympathetic to his anger and desperation, wondered what the grave price of his action might be.

The barn door burst open. A boy stood silhouetted in the grey half-light.

'They're here, you must all come now!' It was Klaus, one of the younger students.

'Who's here?' Hermann asked, his heart racing. He could guess who Klaus meant.

'Police.'

The boys stood up, each stiff with nerves. They followed Klaus across the frosted fields up to the main house. Hermann's heart sank when he saw them: two large, black, covered trucks lined with Gestapo officers. The Gross Breesen students and staff were gathered together in front of the house, wide-eyed with fear. Hermann and the boys from the cowshed joined the group.

Bondy approached one of the officers.

'Please, whatever it is you are here for, I'm sure we can—'

'Silence, you swine!' bellowed the officer. He shoved Bondy backwards into the group. The students were stunned; no-one had ever spoken to their headmaster with such vitriol. Hermann watched Bondy's brow furrow and fall with despair. A few of the younger students began to cry.

Then the officer addressed the group. 'Do any of you know why we are here?'

No-one spoke.

'Anyone at all?'

A few students shook their heads.

'No, we don't know why you're here,' one of the older students said quietly.

The officer gave a nod, and one of his men walked swiftly to the student who had spoken and dealt him a heavy blow to the side of his head. The student fell to the ground, clutching his ear, and began to weep.

An officer holding a sheet of paper stepped forward and began calling out names. Looking around, Hermann realised they were the names of the boys who were 18 years and older, along with the adult men on staff.

'Pollnow!'

Hermann stood forward. The officer pointed to the group of men already called, who stood separate from the rest of the group. Each name was called until all the Gross Breeseners were divided into three groups: men 18 and over, boys under 18, and women and girls. Each group was led away to a different part of the house and locked up under guard. No-one breathed a word.

Hours passed and the students could do nothing but listen as the Gestapo officers jeered and bellowed their vile words through the hallways. They invited local farmers into the grounds, armed with axes, sledgehammers and years of pent-up aggression for the 'Jew farm' and its inhabitants. The students listened as the officers and farmers, mad with rage and alcohol, smashed through windows and furniture, set fire to bookcases, ornaments and statues. One of them axed the grand piano to pieces. They ransacked the Torah cabinet, snatched the Torah, lacerated it to bits and threw the remains on the dung heap outside. They broke into Bondy's office, emptied his liquor cabinet and toasted to the school's decimation.

It was late afternoon when the younger boys, women and girls were released from their guarded rooms. They stumbled over scorched books and shards of glass. They realised that the men over 18 were gone. No explanation was given, there was no sign or trace of where they might have been taken. Even the telephone wire had been cut. Those left could do nothing but wait in Gross Breesen's ruins and imagine in terror what had become of the disappeared.

*

On the whole, we were fairly ignorant of what was going on. We were confused, and then we were ordered—we were all in our dirty outfits from the cowshed—to change and come back. Just to take practically nothing with us. So I went up there, had a wash, put a pair of jeans on, a shirt, my boots, and then they put us in the lorry and drove us to Breslau, to the big police compound. By that time it was probably in the afternoon. They put us in the cellars there, we stayed there overnight. We didn't get any [explanation], *nothing was said. Nothing was said amongst us, either, we didn't sort of… it was a complete, how would I say. Disinformation, or no information at all.*

In the morning, hundreds of Jews were assembled in the courtyard of the prison. Those who had proof of immediate immigration were discharged. The rest of us were marched through the streets of Breslau, watched by thousands of jeering and abusive Germans.[19] *They made us march to the station and we were then put into the old carriages and each carriage had police. We were then still under police protection, as it were. The train then went slowly to Weimar, and then the guards were changed. I remember our guard saying, 'We are now handing you over to the Gestapo; we're no longer responsible for you'. We were driven out onto the station and again we weren't allowed to hold our heads up, we had to have our heads down against the wall then in groups, where they tapped, each group rushed into covered trucks and were driven up to the camp.*

Well, when we got there, it was a big parade ground. It was November, half-dark, all I remember is that we had to stand up for many hours because they said that the facilities weren't ready to take us or something. Quite a few people, especially elderly, couldn't stand up for that long time. Hours. Finally, we were allotted to barracks, wooden barracks and that's where we stayed. Day after day. Separated from the main camp where other prisoners, non-Jewish prisoners, communists, and Jehovah's witnesses and other criminal types—other prisoners—but we had nothing to do with them.

Except when we got there, yes, I forgot. We all had to have our hair shaved off. They did that before we went to the barracks later on in the day.

I was 18 at the time.

5

As warmer months approach, I return to Mum's house to help her sort through decades' worth of accumulated stuff in preparation for her move. It's the house I spent my late childhood and teen years in, and when I walk through the front door and down the hall the walls are porous with the smell and feel of those times. The old wooden floorboards, the lingering air of Mum's percolated coffee and toast from this morning, the sweet scent of jasmine from the backyard. These home smells have a transportive quality that allows me, for a moment, to convene with my young self and retrace her steps. I walk through the living room to the bright open kitchen where Mum sits reading the newspaper, the radio tuned to classical. We hug, she puts another pot of coffee on. I stand on the weathered wooden deck looking out over the small backyard. Next door's gumtree sways slowly in the late afternoon breeze. I inhale the strong smell of the blooming jasmine growing up one side of the shed in the far corner of the yard. The coffee pot gurgles and sputters and Mum pours it into two ceramic mugs. We sit together at the dining table.

'We need to sort through the study,' she says.

'I know, I'm sorry. Most of the stuff is mine.' When I moved out, I left a trail of books, photo albums, random folders full of half-finished stories and forgotten notes, bags of orphaned phone cords and skeletons of old mobile phones. The kind of stuff that is guarded from being thrown out by an invisible force—procrastination, maybe, or sentimentality. The pantry's insides are strewn across the kitchen bench; newspaper-covered glasses and vases sit in rows on the floor; the fridge has been cleared of magnets, flyers, photos, and is now a blank, clean silver. Slowly the whole house will be hollowed out until there's nothing left that is familiar, nothing but those memories in the walls.

I step into the study, open the blinds and window, let the afternoon in. Beneath the window is a stack of unopened heavy cardboard boxes that belong to Harry. They were bequeathed to Mum when he and Lynn moved down to Kiama and have sat in this room untouched ever since. I lift one and move it to the floor in the centre of the room.

'What's in here? Rocks?' I say as I rip through the tape and prise the box open. It's full to the brim with old books, pages musty and coloured by time. *A Brief History of the Third Reich*; *Bertolt Brecht's Berlin*; *The Weimar Years*; *Jewish High Society in Old Regime Berlin*; *Holocaust*. I push the box to the side and grab another. This one isn't as heavy. I open it and find a thick stack of manila folders, loose sheets of paper and newspaper cuttings. I pick up the first manila folder, which someone has labelled *Holocaust* in pink highlighter, underlined twice. Inside the folder is a collection of photocopied newspaper articles, some copied two or three times each. I scan the first one. It's from the late 1990s and is written by a Sydney resident who used to work in the

Auschwitz crematorium. It's titled 'Auschwitz: truth too painful to believe'. The author was a political prisoner and his job was to install electricity in the four gas chambers and, later, fix and reinstall broken wires and cables that were ripped apart by people while they were being gassed. Why would Harry photocopy this article three times? Perhaps he knew the author, but Harry was never at Auschwitz so this is unlikely. The article is sickening, I feel a wave of queasiness as I read. There is something deeply jarring about the everyday electrical maintenance required in a gas chamber. Maybe Harry thought so too. I read that this man gave his testimony at the Nuremberg Trials. The article is written in response to the denialism of a German-born Australian and renowned Holocaust revisionist, Fredrick Toben.

Mum enters the study holding her coffee mug and leans against the desk. She asks me what I've found.

'God, Mum, look at this. Have you heard of Fredrick Toben?'

'Isn't he that Nazi from Adelaide?'

'Yeah, that's him. This article is horrific.' I pass it to her to read.

'Don't, Tess. I can't read that stuff. It's too awful.'

I put the article back with the others.

'Did Harry ever speak to you about Buchenwald?'

Mum pauses, thinking. 'No, not that I can remember. Mum always told us not to bring it up. I suppose he saw no need to speak to his kids about it.'

'Did you ever ask?'

'No.'

I continue sifting through the boxes. Among the cuttings is an article about Harry's relative Ilse Rosenthal-Schneider, who was a student of Albert Einstein's. I recently watched a television series that dramatised Einstein's life, and here was a real person, a relative of Harry's, who was taught by him. So often this history feels far away when really it's deceptively close, hidden in plain sight.

After dinner, Mum's phone rings. We look at each other; it's late for someone to call.

'Hi, Lynn,' says Mum. 'Is everything okay?'

I hear Lynn's muffled voice but can't catch what she's saying. I watch Mum's face fall.

'Oh dear,' Mum says. She glances at me. 'Oh dear. Should I come now?'

Mum eventually hangs up the phone. 'Dad's in hospital. He had bad stomach pains, so Lynn called the ambulance. They're keeping him overnight. I said we would go down tomorrow.'

'Of course,' I reply.

'Poor Dad,' Mum says. Her face is pained.

Neither Mum nor I sleep well. I can't turn my mind off. I am distracted by encroaching thoughts of Harry distressed, disoriented in a strange hospital ward. I worry for Lynn, that the weight of this will be too much for her to bear.

Morning comes quickly, imperceptibly. My room is filled with grey light. Somewhere close by, a lawn mower rips through the calm air. I get up. Mum is already in the kitchen drinking a coffee and holding her phone, texting. I can tell she is steeped in worry. We leave for the South Coast almost immediately.

We take the route through Menai. The road is shadowed on either side by tall, spindly forest. The car hums. Out of the silence, Mum begins to speak.

'I keep thinking about this memory. I'm always reminded

of it when I drive near Mount Ousley: the fog. I hate driving through fog.'

She pauses.

'We were at the snow one year, at Charlotte Pass. I was cross-country skiing with Dad, and all of a sudden a whiteout came over us. Just descended in seconds and, honestly, you couldn't see a centimetre in front of you. Of course, I began to cry and scream out for Dad. I was only young then, maybe 12 or 13. It is really the most terrifying thing, to have your eyes wide open and only see white. Anyway, I didn't know we were on the edge of a huge drop. They didn't rope off cliffs in those days like they do now. Suddenly, I felt a hand grab me and pull me backwards. It was Dad, of course. And I remember he was so calm, while I was so distraught.'

She chuckled. 'It was like nothing had happened, like he could see perfectly clearly through the white. Nothing terrified him. Nothing.'

We arrive at the hospital midmorning. We sign in and are shown to the ward. Lynn has been there all night. Harry is sitting quietly in his bed, a cannula in his right arm, nodding in and out of sleep. Relief fills me, and Mum too, to see that he is calm. Lynn gets up and hugs Mum and me, says thanks for coming.

Lynn says he is being kept in under observation, but he should be okay and he'll be discharged tomorrow. Mum and I pull up two chairs and sit next to him, while Lynn goes out to get some air.

In the ward there's no television, no distraction, nothing. We sit next to Harry for a few hours. He falls asleep and wakes again twice. Mum says to the nurse when she comes to check on him that he'll be fine: he's spent his whole life working in hospitals.

'You okay, Dad?' says Mum.

He looks at her with a forlorn gaze. 'I'm finished, you know.'

'What do you mean?'

'My memory, it's all gone. I'm going mad.'

Mum pauses and glances at me. 'You're not going mad. You've got an infection and you're here to get some treatment, but you'll be home soon.'

'Where are my parents?' he asks.

Mum pauses again. 'They're dead, Dad. They died a long time ago.'

'Are there any Germans here?'

'In this hospital? I don't think so.'

'The Nazis ... are they here?'

'No, Dad. No Nazis here.'

We stay at the hospital all day. I watch as patients leave and arrive, as nurses finish up and begin shifts. The constant beeping of machines and monitors is enough to send anyone mad. Late afternoon eventually seeps in through the far window, soft gold. Mum offers to stay the night but Lynn assures her that she'll be fine. She will stay until Harry goes to sleep, then go back to the flat to feed Charlie and get some rest herself.

'Bye, Dad, we'll see you soon.'

'Where are you going?'

'Home, back to Sydney.'

'You don't live here?'

'No, and neither do you. You're just visiting until you feel better.'

'Okay.' He nods.

'Bye, Harry.' I lean down and kiss his cheek. 'See you soon.'

Mum and I are exhausted on the drive home. Hospital wards

deplete all energy; it is eaten up by worry and static helplessness. Individually, we are hoping that tomorrow will be better, that Harry will wake and feel like himself again, but of this hope neither Mum nor I are confident.

Excerpt from email correspondence with Buchenwald Memorial archive, 13 November 2020.

Dear Tess,

Your grandfather was taken to Buchenwald Concentration Camp in context of the November pogrom in 1938.[20] *Nine thousand, eight hundred and forty-five Jewish people had been deported to Buchenwald during the wave of arrests that followed. Despite the importance of this mass deportation for the persecution of the Jewish Germans we only have minimal personal related information about most of the victims. Upon their arrival in Buchenwald they were registered in special records that were separated from the common camp registry. Unfortunately, these special records provide only minimal information such as name, prisoner number and date of death or release. Further details (such as date of birth, place of residence etc.) are not included.*

Coming back to the information that we're able to provide you with we can state the following: Hermann Ludwig Pollnow was brought to Buchenwald Concentration Camp on 12 November 1938. Upon his arrival he was registered under the inmate number 28382, as you already know. He and the other victims of the November pogrom were placed in a 'Special Pogrom Camp' on the west side of the roll call ground, a place where the terror of the SS reached its most extreme form. Fortunately, your grandfather was released from there on 4 December 1938. I'm afraid that we don't have further information about his fate.

The parade ground at Buchenwald camp was quiet. Freezing wind whistled through hollow trees. Lines and lines of arrested men stood still and terrified. Hermann was one of them, but he was impossible to pick out from the crowd. They stood for hours, for longer than the sun, until their knees began to tremble. Some elderly men fell to the ground, unable to support themselves any longer. They were taken away. Stomachs rumbled as last meals disappeared into thick vaporous exhales, devoured by shaking muscles. Time stagnated. There were no signs of relief or relent for the imprisoned, who could do nothing but stand still and pray their legs did not buckle beneath them.

Finally, when it seemed as if days had passed, they were assigned barracks. The Gross Breesen students and a handful of staff were kept away from the other prisoners. They were not assigned to work groups like the rest. They were classified as temporary prisoners; their fates were as yet undecided, though they were not given a shred of information.

Like all the other prisoners, the Gross Breeseners were forced into a new life of perpetual starvation and thirst;

were denied medical treatment for illness; were supplied with one forsaken latrine for thousands of prisoners; faced day after day of stasis and uncertainty; and were subjected to horrific beatings, degradation and violence from the SS guards, who were often young, fuelled by substances and armed with years of poisonous indoctrination. The guards would descend on the barracks late at night, yank the sleeping prisoners from their bunks and rob them, beat them senseless, sometimes to death.[21] The Gross Breeseners were charged with the task of collecting the corpses of prisoners who had died overnight from such incidents, or from malnourishment or disease. Hermann was one of those tasked with collections. He carried bodies, labelled them and transported them to the wash house. What happened to the bodies after that was someone else's task.

The Gross Breesen group were imprisoned at Buchenwald for nearly one month. This was enough time for their teenage minds to be permanently etched with what they witnessed. Back home, all efforts were made by friends and relatives, anyone with connections to the imprisoned Gross Breesen staff and students, to secure their passage out of Germany. The only reason a prisoner was released at that time, in the wake of Kristallnacht, was if they could prove their intent to leave their home country forever.

Attaining emigration papers was no easy task. The German bureaucracy demanded strict adherence to rules and procedures regardless of the circumstance, which in the case of each prisoner was a matter of life and death. Acquiring affidavits, visas, necessary funds and all the required papers within the timeframes was so exceedingly difficult to achieve that the determination of a person's fate was like a lottery—a high-stakes game of chance. What the Gross Breeseners had on their side was their experience in agriculture, training in farm labour and capacity for physical work. In the eyes of the Nazis who processed the Gross Breesen students into the camp, the idea that a Jew could be a farmer and manual labourer was so preposterous that upon registering at Buchenwald the students were laughed at. Overseas, though, an emigrant's agricultural skills were prized above all else. Without this small advantage, they would have been thrown into the pit with their campmates, families, friends and the other millions, into the lottery of survival.

> *I had a feeling of extreme abandonment. I was abandoned and terribly lonely. Even though we had there some of the Gross Breesen boys with us, but we were not … we were probably in a state of shock. We couldn't comprehend what was happening. And certainly, even at that time we didn't think of what was going to happen to us, that we were going to be killed or nothing. We just, the whole process was just incomprehensible to us. We didn't get any encouragement or any signs of hope or, you know, so um. I think that individually we were very lonely.*
>
> *I don't think they* [my parents] *found out what happened … in December they decided to release some or … I think we were allowed to send a pre-printed card, 'We are here. We are well', and that's it. But then later, they started to call our names every day, for people that were going to be released. They gave us a postcard and we had to write home for them to send money*

to pay the fare back. I think that might have been the first time they realised where I was. Or where we were. And when the names were called out every day, we went into the main camp. They cleaned us up a bit, and [we] *stayed in the normal barracks there for the night and were then discharged or let out under guard and walked down by the guard to the station.*

Upon their release, the prisoners were ordered into the administrative building at the centre of the camp. In exchange for their release, they were forced to renounce their German citizenship and were ordered to leave Germany immediately. They were required to submit themselves to daily checks by the Gestapo and local police to monitor the progression of their emigration plans. Above all, the prisoners were to say nothing to anybody about what they saw and experienced in the camp. Sworn to bitter silence, the prisoners faced reimprisonment or execution if they uttered a word to anyone about their time at Buchenwald.

Hermann walked with stiff legs and a shivering torso alongside the group of released prisoners, his fellow Gross Breeseners. He could not believe what was happening; everything he had witnessed culminated in a thick cloud of incredulity and numbness. Rationality had been manipulated, contradicted; what he thought was the way of the world had been thwarted violently, horrifically.

No prisoner breathed a word, but their questions hung in the air above them unanswered: why were they being released? Who was responsible? What happened to the rest of the Gross Breeseners? Were their families alright? Each boy questioned in silence.

Hermann forced himself to look ahead and distract his mind—so conditioned to looking back, remembering—with stepping one foot in front of the other. Yet his thoughts leaked through this wall of determined repression, with scenes not so easily forgotten. He shivered and pulled his coat tighter across his shaking frame. The winter cold was a torturous affront to his already weakened body. The morning was heavy. Snow blanketed the earth, hardened and unforgiving. He kept his eyes down. The boys learned quickly in the camp to appear invisible, to not draw attention, to avert eyes at all times; to be seen was perilous.

To be on the other side of the fence, away from that hell—was that freedom? To have endured subjection to the excesses of violence, the hideous filthy stench and presence of death, dehumanisation, to have made it out physically unscathed while the rest were left, those who had no money, no papers, no family to advocate for their release—was that freedom? There was no freedom in walking from Buchenwald, knowing what they had left behind. The memories would be with them forever.

Hermann tripped over a surfaced tree root but caught himself before anyone noticed. Tangled in his vision were horsewhips and bare, bloodied hands. Aching bones hunched over a latrine, odour beyond belief, his insides quivering in pain. The engulfing cold and darkness of night, each longer than the last, filled with howls of tortured pain, cries, terror-stricken faces and, from those who did not make it through, deep silence. Hermann looked ahead, focusing on the road, but instead what flashed before him was a cold grey arm hanging out at a sickly angle away from the bunk, early in the morning. The fingers were curled up, withered and blackened. He dragged the lice-infested blanket from the corpse and met a face, eyes cast upwards, mouth hung limp revealing mangled, rotted bottom teeth. With aid from another boy, he pulled the body from the barrack, labelled and loaded it onto the wagon, then searched the barrack for more dead.

Hermann shook his head, erased the thoughts and brought himself back to the present moment. He heard shouting from behind him but did not dare look back. No-one around him broke rank, one foot in front of the other. He heard maniacal screams, presumably from one of the guards. Another smaller voice pleaded. Hermann kept walking, straining to hear any flecks of recognition in the prisoner's receding wails as he was dragged back to the camp.

The rest of the walk was silent except for the crunch of snow beneath their shoes and the occasional spitting and taunting of the guards. Light rain began to fall. Snow coated the thick wall of trees that lined the road, piling up on each branch and weighing them down. On the ground, it melted into the mud. They traipsed through the brown sludge, leaving boot marks that would soon disappear beneath a new layer of snow.

In Weimar, relics of Kristallnacht were visible everywhere; rubble from burnt shops still plagued the streets. Civilians walked around it. This was the first time the prisoners realised that the attack on Gross Breesen was not isolated. The gravity of the pogrom began to descend onto the shoulders of each of them.

The SS guards were quick and sharp with their final words: any word of what the prisoners saw and they would be immediately arrested and sent back to the camp with no chance of release, or they would be shot. A truck arrived from the camp, the guards filed in and drove away, back to where they had come from, and left Hermann and the other released prisoners at the station, back in civilised society as if nothing had happened. Around them, Weimar citizens went about their days. They did not hide their stares, for the prisoners were unmistakable with their identically shaved heads. The citizens knew where they had come from; Buchenwald Concentration Camp had been part of their municipality since July 1937, when the first prisoners arrived and were forced to build the camp themselves. In the wake of Kristallnacht, it was not safe for Jews to be out in the street, at the hands of emboldened Nazi supporters and Brownshirts.[22] Those who were to return to Gross Breesen before finally heading home, Hermann among them, made their way swiftly into the station, speaking to no-one, averting their gaze at all times.

*Hermann Pollnow, prisoner number 28382,
4 December 1938.*

6

7 December 1938

Dear Mutzi,

Your letter just arrived and you can imagine how happy we were to read something comprehensive about you. Above all, we are very happy for you that you are going on vacation,[23] *hopefully that will happen soon.*

I have ordered the birth certificate, but I haven't received it yet. For the time being, I will send you another one, but it probably won't be enough. I will also include 10 RM. There are many more things to tell you, but I'd prefer to wait until you are here in person. In the meantime, I'll limit myself to only writing about important things.

It's not going so great with the clinic, in part because I'm not allowed to advertise. By the way, I'm also working as a substitute doctor in the Israelite Hospital in Elsässer Strasse ...

Mutti's condition is basically unchanged, but certainly not better. I spend much more time at home, whenever I can, just like I used to in the past ...

Oma is doing fine; she might have even sent you a parcel already...

I will send you the correct birth certificate as soon as it arrives. Hopefully, the formal requirements of issuing your proof of identity won't delay the start of your vacation. To be on the safe side, I'll send you the confirmation of the additional [Jewish] *first name for the local police.*

1000 greetings and kisses from Mutti and Vati.

When I try to imagine Hermann's final days at his parents' flat before departure to Holland I am struck by a kind of block, a void in my vision and feeling mind. I can't imagine the pain. The letters that surround this moment convey administrative details of correct names and identity documents and fees. The despair is unsaid. In the month that Hermann was imprisoned in Buchenwald, Max and Edith received no news, no hint at where he might be. They knew he had been arrested but not where he'd been taken. Rumours abounded but nothing was concretely known until finally, miraculously, they received word that he was to be released from Buchenwald Camp and required the fare for the train ticket home. Emigration plans for the Gross Breesen students were already in motion prior to Kristallnacht, but it was advocacy from Bondy's influential circle and relentless lobbying for the permits that ensured the students' release. I can string together a chronological sequence of Hermann's imprisonment, release, return home and escape from Germany from the records of those who lived through it alongside him. His good fortune is almost unbelievable; he was granted a permit to enter Holland and so was allowed to escape certain death. If Max did not have the money to send him to Gross Breesen in the first place, if the Gross Breesen students did not have access to Bondy's influence and international connections, they might have been arrested and imprisoned with no hope of release. The Pollnows were not wealthy people, but they had enough to secure their son's escape. That a certain amount of money could buy one passage basically anywhere is unsurprising, and yet the grave unfairness hangs heavy over this story.

Uncertainty would have poisoned all aspects of life for Max and Edith during this period. Perpetual unknowing, of their son's whereabouts, of their own fates, of what could possibly come next; I cannot imagine it. Life would have continued on, despite these insurmountable chasms. Max would have continued treating patients, Ella would have continued to visit Edith, Edith would have continued to live through each day despite not knowing how to endure such cruelty. In her mind, I imagine, nothing was more important than getting her son out of Germany. Despite whatever might happen to her and Max, Hermann's safety was all that mattered.

The Pollnows' new flat in Johannisstrasse was smaller than they were used to, but had just enough room for Fräulein Selma to continue as Edith's live-in carer. Now that the renovations were finally complete, their living conditions were not quite so dire. The cracks in the walls were repaired, the light fixtures and pipes replaced. The lounge room could only fit their two leather armchairs and Max's writing secretaire, which still seemed too large for space. Yet in the soft worn leather and aged wood were memories, the scent of old life salvaged; the rest had to be sold. There was no second bedroom for Hermann.

Max sat in an armchair reading the newspaper, his cigar poised above the ashtray. He glanced at the front door every few minutes, waiting for the sound of his son's footsteps on the landing outside the flat. *Any minute now*, he thought.

Finally, quick footsteps, followed by a knock on the door.

Max leaped to his feet and flung open the door.

'Mutzi!' he exclaimed, pulling Hermann to his chest. He felt frail, almost unfamiliar.

Max felt Hermann stiffen then yield to his embrace. Max had never held his son like this, never showed such outward affection. But they held each other for a long time; neither man realised how deeply he had missed the other. Max pulled back, stood up straight and placed his hands atop Hermann's shoulders, regarding his son for the first time in months. Hermann was much thinner than usual and his eyes were encircled by dark shadows, much like Max's. He put one hand on Hermann's crown and felt the prickles of new hair, already beginning to grow back thick and dark.

'At least they gave you a proper haircut,' said Max.[24] 'Come on, come inside. Mutti won't believe her eyes.'

Hermann opened the bedroom door. He saw Edith bundled up under a blanket, hair gently lining her face, eyes open but slightly unfocused. Then she saw him.

'Mutzi!' she wailed.

He went to his mother and held her, kissed her cheeks. 'Hello, Mutti,' he said. 'I've missed you.'

'And I you, my darling, more than you could ever imagine.'

Hermann noticed how pale she looked, how much her illness had taken hold since he last saw her. She began to weep.

Max came to the door. 'Oma is on her way now.'

'My dear Mutzilein!' cried Ella, squeezing Hermann tightly. 'You look dreadful. What did they do to your lovely hair?'

'It will grow back, Oma,' said Hermann. Oma gave him another hug.

'I've brought you some treats for your journey. Just a few things to sustain you for the train ride.'

She pulled out chocolate, cigarettes and Hermann's favourite sweets. All were quiet as they remembered Hermann's imminent departure. He was to board the train to Holland where he would await confirmation of his passage to Australia. There was no mention of the possibility of Oma, Max and Edith joining Hermann at his distant destination. The alternative prospect, reality, was too painful to voice.

'Nearly ready?' Max asked his son. The morning of departure had arrived.

'Yes,' Hermann replied.

Max nodded and Hermann walked to his parents' bedroom where Edith was lying awake, looking out the window.

'My Mutzi,' she said when she saw him, and began to weep. 'My boy!'

Hermann sat beside her and clasped her hands in his, wanting desperately to tell her that everything was alright and he would see her soon. And Edith, looking at her brave, grown-up child, wanted desperately to tell Hermann that she and Max would always be there to protect him and that, somehow, they would find a way to follow him across the world. Neither could bear that this was the last time their hands would be entwined.

'I love you, Mutti,' said Hermann. 'I will always be thinking of you.'

'Oh, how I love you, Mutzi,' said Edith. 'You will be all I think of for the rest of my life.'

Max stood in the bedroom doorway. 'We should be going. You can't miss your train.'

Hermann held his mother and kissed her forehead then stood up, shaking slightly, and left the room. He followed his father down the steps of the flat, out into the freezing morning.

On the station platform, the group of Gross Breeseners travelling to Holland were gathered, clutching their trunks and wearing thick winter coats. Passengers were boarding, kissing loved ones, those going on a holiday alongside those saying goodbye to their families forever. Guards blew their whistles and more people began to board. Hermann and Max stood together. They looked like the same man, decades apart.

'Try to call as soon as you get to Amsterdam,' said Max. 'I'm sure Bondy will see to it.'

Hermann nodded.

'We will write, of course. Make sure you pay attention to the numbers on each page, so you know if any have been taken out. Well ...'

Max looked at his son, now 18, and remembered the small boy he used to take with him on house calls, in shorts and shirts so small they might have been a doll's clothes. He remembered young Mutzi's thick ringlets, identical to his own, the cheeky grin he wore constantly as a boy. He remembered teaching him to read and do arithmetic, teaching him to ski, practising his Spanish after school. Max felt a deep pain in the pit of his stomach for all the days and evenings he did not spend with Hermann because of work, because he thought there would be plenty of time to spend with his son in his later years. This vision of the future was gone, and his eyes filled with tears.

'Make sure you write to us every week. We want to hear about everything. Do you promise?'

'Yes, Vati.'

'Good. Now, make sure you work hard, wherever you go. Never lose your good character and humour. That's the most important advice I can give you. I hope that we will be together again one day, when this is all over.'

Max pulled Hermann to his chest and both men began to cry. 'We will always be thinking of you. I love you, Mutzi.'

'I love you too, Vati.'

Max faced his son and took a breath. 'Never come back to Germany. This is not our country anymore.'

Max watched as Hermann boarded the train and disappeared into the packed carriage. He waited on the platform until the train jolted, hissed and slowly began to move. The moment's heaviness constricted his chest and he had to remind himself to breathe. The terror of his own fate was nothing compared to the worry he felt for Hermann's safety. He had done everything he could. There was nothing left to do but wait and hope.

Max stood on the platform until the train was out of sight. Then he tightened his coat around his chest and made his way home.

*

Did you discuss your parents leaving with you?

No. It was never discussed. There was no chance that my father could. He didn't have enough money to go, for example, to Australia, where you could go if you had a certain amount of money. Many other countries you could practically buy a permit. He couldn't go to America; he couldn't work anywhere at that time. He was about 55. Wasn't old. But that was never discussed. And so we, the people that were in the concentration camp, in Gross Breesen, we got a permit to go to Holland. To Wieringen, which at that time was in the Wieringermeer, reclaimed from the ocean and transformed into farmland. Nieuwesluis was a Jewish Zionist farm.

When was the last time you saw your parents?

It was a day before I left for Holland. So, I went from Gross Breesen to Berlin, and stayed at my parents' flat, and as I said, my mother was in bed. My father took me to the station with my trunk and we all assembled, a few boys from Gross Breesen, and went to Amsterdam, I suppose. That's the last time I saw them.

It was very… hard, I think. In moments like that, there's a lot to say but nothing much is said. My father gave me more advice. He hoped to see us, but [there was] *not any mechanism how that would come about. I think my parents, many times, said that they would not survive Hitler's end, but I would. That they were quite sure that they wouldn't.*

So I never, as I said, I never saw them again.

Excerpt from the restitution claim of Dr Harry Peters to the German government, 29 August 2000:

a) Altonaer Strasse 8

Some years ago (1954?) I submitted an inventory for my restitution claim which listed in detail all the furnishings etc. in that unit. In particular I listed the contents of the waiting room and the surgery (consulting/treating room). My father was a surgeon and he had a considerable number of surgical instruments and equipment including, [what] *was at that time, a very modern complex examination/treatment table. All instruments were kept in glasses in steel cabinets. There was also a mobile operating light in the surgery.*

b) Schillerpromenade 12, Oberschöneweide

1) Wohnung (on Third Floor)
2 Bedroom
1 Dining room
1 Lounge room

1 Maid's room
1 Kitchen
1 Bathroom/toilet
1 Verandah

The flat/unit was about the same size as the one at Hansaplatz (minus the waiting room and the consulting room). Also it did not have two corridors and no storage room next to the kitchen.

1) Surgery (on Ground Floor)
Consisted of:

1 Waiting room which had only the usual chairs, table for magazines, light fittings and a carpet.
1 Consulting/treatment room which had the same contents and was of the same size as in the Altonaer Strasse establishment.
1 Store room where some medical equipment, medications, dressings, sterilising solutions and stationery was kept.
1 Toilet

2) Johannisstrasse 8

As stated in my last letter to you, I only stayed a few days in that unit prior to my departure to Holland and my memory is a bit blurred. However the unit consisted of the rooms as listed in your letter. The contents of the consulting room had not changed. I cannot clearly remember a waiting room but I think that a few chairs were present in a small room. (I slept for two nights in the consulting room on a couch!) The bedroom had the same furnishings and the corner room which was not big only contained half of the previous lounge and dining furnishings.

I must thank you for your continuing effort to pursue this claim and I hope that the above information will be of help to you. Kind regards.

Sincerely, Dr Harry Peters

Inventory for restitution claim by Dr Harry Peters.

Contents of apartment occupied by Dr Max Israel Pollnow and Edith Sara Pollnow at Schillerpromenade 12 Oberschöneweide.

Lounge room:

One Blüthner grand piano (black)[25]
One oval lounge room table (rosewood)
One mahogany writing secretaire
Two leather lounge chairs
Four lounge room chairs (oak)
One library bookcase (with glass doors) made of oak
One Persian carpet
Light fittings and paintings

Dining room:

One dining table for eight people made of solid oak

Eight dining-room chairs made of oak

One antique sideboard hand carved made of solid oak

One glass cabinet with glass doors and oak frame for glasses and art objects

One large Persian carpet

Silver cutlery and crockery (Rosenthal porcelain) for eight people

Römer glasses, silver dishes, silver candelabra (two)

One crystal chandelier

Main bedroom occupied by my parents:

One double bed made of oak (blond)

Two bedside tables (oak)

One double door wardrobe made of solid oak (blond)

Two bedside chairs

One crystal chandelier

One woollen carpet

Second bedroom:

One bed

One writing desk

One wardrobe

One bookcase

Contents of surgery and waiting room:

One big desk with four drawers and made of solid oak

One desk chair

One steel and glass (60 x 60cm) instrumental cupboard

One steriliser (water bath)

One surgical examination table with stirrups and hydraulic

height adjustments
One mobile operating light for surgical procedures
Full set of surgical instruments
One double door glassed-in bookcase to hold all medical books, journals etc.

Waiting room:

Eight chairs
Table
Carpet
Light fittings

Not listed in detail:

All bed linen, towels, kitchen utensils etc.

Letter from Professor Curt Bondy to Gertrude van Tijn, Secretary of the Werkdorp Nieuwesluis and Jewish Labour Foundation, 24 December 1938.

Dear Mrs van Tijn,

I have received news of my boys who have now arrived in Wieringen, and I honestly owe you and your colleagues my heartfelt thanks for all that you have done and continue to do for us.

With great joy and deep gratitude I learned after my trip [to Buchenwald] *of the different emigration possibilities for the Gross Breeseners, and above all, the chance to stay in Holland during the waiting period. It was especially pleasing to us that the boys could continue to learn their profession and have good accommodation during this time. We sincerely hope that the boys' stay in Wieringen won't last long and that they can soon get to their destinations.*

A group of them are to go to Hyde Farmlands, the farm put at our disposal near Richmond, Virginia. The preparatory work (light and water installations, etc.) is in full progress. Five boys are already at the farm, and the latest news from the USA gives us reason to hope that the immigration problems that still persist will be cleaned up in the near future. My recent visit to the Dutch Consulate General in Berlin proved to me that the project is being pursued with serious interest.

Among the boys who are being proposed now are a number who are to go to Australia. This project is similar to the one in Virginia in that about 30 boys and girls are to be sent to [a] *farm ... and we hope that our agronomist* [Scheier] *and his wife, who have been in this work for many years, will become the administrators there. The last cable from Sydney was quite positive, and the permits are expected soon.*

So we hope that this group, too—if you give them permission to come to Wieringen—will occupy their places there only for a short time.

If changes have occurred in our proposal lists, it is because a small number of our people haven't yet returned [from Buchenwald], *for others sudden emigration possibilities arise, and the list of those going to Denmark is not yet quite settled. And finally, sudden emigration possibilities are sometimes found for the parents, who then take their children with them, or hopes of emigration turn out to be unfounded. So please don't be angry when changes occur now and then in our proposals.*

According to the news we have received, we can suggest five more people who can perhaps be sent to Wieringen. We request that you wait a few more days on this matter, until we have definite news about the accommodation in Denmark.

In expressing to you once again my heartfelt thanks for your admirable work, with kind regards, I am,

Yours faithfully,
[handwritten] *Bo.*

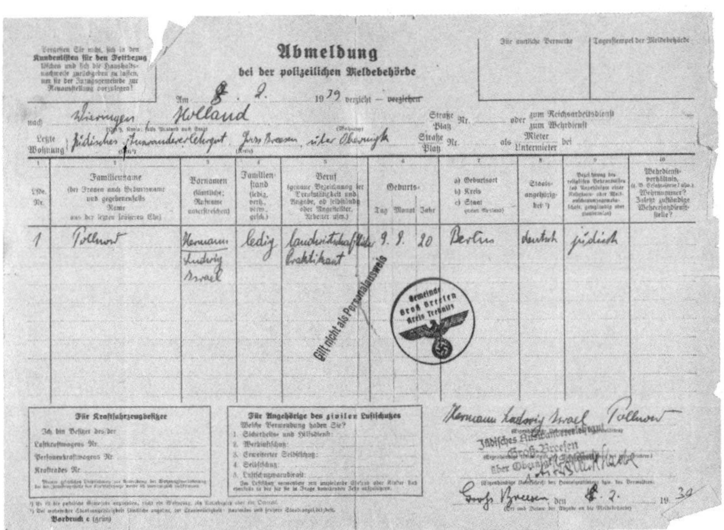

Abmeldung
bei der polizeilichen Meldebehörde

Vergessen Sie nicht, sich in den **Kundenlisten für den Fettbezug** löschen und sich die Haushaltsnachweise zurückgeben zu lassen, um sie der Zuzugsgemeinde zur Neuausstellung vorzulegen!

Für amtliche Vermerke | Tagesstempel der Meldebehörde

Am 8. 2. 1939 verzieht — ~~verzogen~~

nach Wieringen Holland — Straße/Platz Nr. — oder zum Reichsarbeitsdienst / zum Wehrdienst

Letzte Wohnung: Jüdisches Auswandererlehrgut Gross Breesen, über Obernigk — Straße/Platz Nr. — als Mieter/Untermieter bei

Lfde. Nr.	Familienname (bei Frauen auch Geburtsname und gegebenenfalls Name aus der letzten früheren Ehe)	Vornamen (sämtliche; Rufname unterstreichen)	Familienstand (ledig, verh., verw., gesch.)	Beruf (genaue Bezeichnung der Erwerbstätigkeit und Angabe, ob selbständig oder Angestellter, Arbeiter usw.)	Geburts- Tag	Monat	Jahr	a) Geburtsort b) Kreis c) Staat	Staatsangehörigkeit	Bezeichnung des religiösen Bekenntnisses	Wehrdienstverhältnis
1	Pollnow	Hermann Ludwig Israel	ledig	landwirtschaftlicher Praktikant	9.	9.	20	Berlin	deutsch	jüdisch	

Gilt nicht als Personalausweis

Gemeinde Groß Breesen Kreis Trebnitz

Für Kraftfahrzeugbesitzer
Ich bin Besitzer des/der
Lastkraftwagens Nr.
Personenkraftwagens Nr.
Kraftrades Nr.

Für Angehörige des zivilen Luftschutzes
Welche Verwendung haben Sie?
1. Sicherheits- und Hilfsdienst:
2. Werkluftschutz:
3. Erweiterter Selbstschutz:
4. Selbstschutz:
5. Luftschutzwarndienst:

Hermann Ludwig Israel Pollnow

Jüdisches Auswandererlehrgut Groß-Breesen über Obernigk

Groß Breesen, den 8. 2. 1939

Vordruck c (grün)

Police registration paper, indicating that Hermann Pollnow changed address from Gross Breesen to Wieringen, Holland, on 8 February 1939.

The refugees exhaled with relief as the train crossed the border into Holland. They were finally rid of the German guards who, if it were up to them, would have arrested them all and sent them straight back to imprisonment. The atmosphere changed; they felt momentarily lighter. Out the window great expanses of green fields speckled with quaint homesteads on the horizon.

They travelled to Amsterdam first, to the Central Jewish Committee, where the students were recorded and checked before travelling north to Wieringen. Werkdorp Nieuwesluis was their destination, an agricultural training and transit camp for Jews fleeing Germany, about 30 kilometres from the town of Alkmaar. The Werkdorp was located on a stretch of land called the Wieringermeer polder, a polder being a feat of Dutch engineering by which land was reclaimed from the sea.[26] Originally the polder was 65 hectares but soon grew to over 360 hectares. What were just recently barracks for the polder workers became barracks for the Werkdorp's trainees. Already the camp was severely overcrowded as refugee numbers surged in the wake of Kristallnacht. More barracks were erected as well as a large community hall built by the early trainees, stables and specialist sheds for metalwork and carpentry. In the new polder soil, flowers flourished and grass grew lush and vibrant green.

The refugees worked out in the fields and garden, raised poultry, and cared for the growing number of cattle, sheep and horses. They were educated in farm machinery, learned how to drive tractors, and made furniture in the carpentry workshop, while in the smithy they shod horses, welded and made fixtures and repairs. The camp was preparing most Jewish refugees for migration to Palestine but there was still a contingent of non-

Zionist Jews, the Gross Breeseners included, who awaited passage elsewhere. The original dream had been to emigrate together, all the Gross Breeseners, and set up a farm overseas identical to their Silesian home. First it was North America—Australia, too, held promise—and for a time it seemed possible that Gross Breesen might be re-established, values and teachings and friendships intact. After Kristallnacht, this dream was quickly extinguished, as the frenzied rush to secure escape by any means thwarted their utopian vision of collective movement. Already the Gross Breeseners were divided. Some got out early with their families; others secured jobs in England; most awaited travel permits for Australia, North and South America and Kenya. The unluckiest were still at Gross Breesen, surrounded by the violent memories of Kristallnacht and the hollow corridors and dormitories that once hummed with the energy of their peers.[27]

The boys were taken to their newly constructed barracks. As they walked through the farm, they saw a group of boys playing football on a far field; they saw students sitting and reading beneath a tree. Four young girls cycled past, their shrieks of laughter trailing behind them. The atmosphere here was different, more relaxed than at Gross Breesen; even in these first hours Hermann observed a much lower regard for routine and discipline.

Inside the barracks, the furniture was sparse: bunks, wash basin, small dining table and four chairs. Someone had dressed the table in a white tablecloth and collected a few flowers in a vase. In the corner of the kitchen bench sat a wireless radio, and a small window looked out onto the shared garden. At the door, Hermann noticed three pairs of large wooden clogs caked in dirt.

They settled in, changed clothes and washed up for dinner. The dining hall was divided into groups and it seemed that these groups kept to themselves. The Gross Breeseners sat together and ate quietly, regarding their new fellows. Hermann wondered for how long this would be their home. It could be weeks or months; nothing was certain. He wondered how long some of the refugees had been here, where they came from, what they had escaped. Despite the turmoil of recent months, the dining hall felt warm and jovial. That night, Hermann slept heavily for the first time in what felt like an age.

Nieuwesluis hut, taken by Hermann Pollnow, 1939.

Days ticked into weeks at the Werkdorp and still no emigration plan was secured. They worked relentlessly, from dawn until the sun slipped beneath the sea line. Focus on work eased the perpetual stress of not knowing where they might end up and the news of deteriorating circumstances back in Germany.

It was maddening to suddenly find their fates dependent on the will of committees and guarantors. Uncertainty for any length of time put a strain on even the most determined mind. Conversations went back and forth between consulates, who could do nothing without sufficient advice from Berlin. The administrative process was labyrinthine and virtually impossible to predict. Hermann and the other Gross Breesen boys pursued their agricultural training because that was their strength. Hermann threw himself into the work, kept his head down and focused on the future. Always the future.

So how did you go about coming to Australia?
Applications were made, at the time not only for ... the scheme was that after 1936 when Hitler's laws, the Nuremberg Laws and all that, organisations were catering to young Jews to emigrate. That was universal, in England, Australia and of course, pitiful few, only very few were taken. Guarantors were found for us—my guarantor was de Vahl Davis—and permits [were] *issued.*[28] *Also to come here as farm workers which helped the selection process, so that all the young people, 21 of us that came from Gross Breesen, all started primarily working on farms. The other Gross Breeseners that did not get out at that time, some* [later] *got*

out to Kenya, the United States, also on farms, training farms in Hyde Park, Virginia, and some went to South America.

Nieuwesluis trainees on a day off in Wieringen, taken by Hermann Pollnow, 1939.

[Undated; presumably April 1939]

My dear Mutzilein!

Last week there was so much to deal with, that I didn't manage to write. Anyway, you are always on my mind, and I read every single one of your reports with great interest. Today, your mother told me that your journey to England would be delayed. This time will pass very quickly though and very soon you will be on the vast sea heading towards your goals! A fabulous time is ahead of you and many people would envy you for that. Enjoy it! We are happy for you that you can explore the world in such a pleasant way. I am looking forward to your reports already.

Yesterday, you would have been so excited. Eventually, after many cold days, the sun was shining and I decided, along with Fräulein Hanni F. and her mother, to go on a trip.[29] *It was so wonderful! We took the train from Zoo station to Potsdam and from there to Sanssouci,*[30] *where we viewed the park. Fräulein H. was very impressed, because she hadn't seen the park before. We ate and drank at the historical mill and took the ship to Wannsee, where we had a coffee. It was a beautiful day, which satisfied all of us. Fräulein H. is a very charming girl, whom I really like. As a little souvenir, I gave her a cute turtle badge. I believe she was very pleased. Her mother is also a very nice woman, who will also eventually come to Australia. Apart from that, there is not much going on. It is always the same.*

Your mother is really impressed by Frau Hanna, the new housemaid. She is very friendly, which is important given Mother's nerves.

Time is passing so quickly.

Enjoy yourself and feel embraced by your old Oma.

For Hermann, letters from family made their absence feel stronger; hearing of their lives and happenings brought into sharp focus all that he was missing. At times, this longing brought about an almost intolerable grief that descended out of nowhere when a thought or memory of his past life appeared and distracted Hermann from his painful reality. Visiting Potsdam on summer holidays with friends, hiking in the forest there or swimming at Wannsee. These brief reminiscences were soon overtaken by the distress of the previous few months, the harsh impossibility of returning to the life he had envisioned since childhood. He knew he was lucky, and he wanted to escape Germany more than anything. But his safety came at a high price, one that was never reconciled.

With spring came a miracle: confirmed passage to Australia on a ship called the SS *Strathallan*. One afternoon close to their departure from Nieuwesluis, a group of students, Hermann included, decided to spend a few hours by the lake. The weather had warmed and the water, though still icy, felt bearable in the beaming midafternoon sun.

Hermann and the other students traipsed across the grass, blankets under their arms and brows sweating. Hermann paused for a moment and watched as the others sprinted towards the lake, glistening and perfect. They picked a patch of grass flat enough to lay out the blankets. The boys unbuttoned their shirts, the girls their blouses and skirts. When they were all lying down facing the lake, Hermann ran in front of the group, camera in hand. A few of the group locked eyes with his lens, while others paid no attention, already engrossed in their books. Hermann joined the group, lay down and closed his eyes. Their conversations melted away as he relented to the breeze, the flies and tickling grass, the sweetness of momentary freedom. Finally, after months of whispers, bargaining and dashed hopes, the Gross Breesen students knew where they were going.

Eventually the heat made the lake impossible to ignore. Hermann stood up, took off his trousers and raced down the grassy dune. Some rushed in and others waded into the shallows, shrieking at the cold water biting their ankles. Hermann ran towards the waterline and dived in, letting the water engulf him fully. Then he floated to the surface and stretched his arms out, felt his lightness, his whole being supported by the lake.

A letter from Hermann Pollnow to Sir Samuel Cohen, founding president of the Australian Jewish Welfare Society. Undated but presumably written in April 1939.

Dear Sir!

I must apologise that I have not written earlier to you and express my hearty thanks for your generosity in giving me a permit. You cannot imagine how thankful I am to you that you have made it possible for me to come to your country. I can assure you that I will do my best to become a good citizen. I am with a group of 22 agricultural practitioners, who will improve your agriculture. It may be that we will go first to a government farm for one or two years. After this time, we will be given a job as a farmhand in the country. But I do not know exactly. I have worked for one year on a farm in Germany. In November, I spent four weeks in Buchenwald, and since February, I've been on a farm in Holland. Last week I was informed about the voyage. We shall leave London on 9 June with the SS Strathallan. *The arrival in Sydney will be on 19 July. Then I shall be very glad to make your acquaintance. Once more I thank you so much for your help and kindness.*

With many regards I am

Yours sincerely,
Hermann Pollnow

7

It was already the first week of May. Time was passing so quickly, and yet it seemed that life was in stasis. When Max was reminded that a year had passed since last spring, he could scarcely believe it. Berlin was changed, and with it, all aspects of his old life. His patients were fewer; he rarely performed surgeries. He spent more time at home now than he ever had, which, he reasoned, was a good thing for Edith. But he missed work sorely. It pained Max to feel useless. The days of a full salary and right to treat all patients were long gone. He still had a handful of regular patients but his work now was a far cry from his days at the AEG. He missed the bustling hospital corridors and his old colleagues and their first flat on Altonaer Strasse, despite the noise and relentless traffic. He missed a lot of things. The stress of finding a new place to live left its mark on Max, as did the financial strain of his acutely diminished income. What little he did earn went to Hermann's boarding fees in Wieringen and, now, Hermann's emigration.

These days nothing was ever certain until it was so, especially any emigration plans that involved multiple moving parts and relied so heavily on the will and charity of foreign governments. Hermann's emigration involved gaining the approval from consulates and the Australian Government, the communications of which often took weeks to progress. Luggage had to be organised and transported, freight fees paid; in fact, payment was seemingly required at every stage of the emigration process. Max paid everything without a second thought. Hermann's departure date for Australia was now fast approaching.

Max was relieved that despite all these upheavals, Hermann had not lost his good character, his determination or his wits. It pained Max to think that his son had to experience the terror of a concentration camp at only 18 years old. It sickened him to think of what Hermann saw, just as it sickened him to recall his own experiences in the Great War. After all his efforts, Hermann still had to endure such a place. Still, he was comforted by the fact that his son would never have to see those sights again.

Hermann was to stay with his cousin Ulla, the eldest daughter of Heinz and Irmgard, and Ulla's husband, Erich, at their house in Maida Vale, London, in the days leading up to departure. From there Hermann would set sail for Australia. Finally, after months that felt like years, plans were in motion.

Letter from Ulla Sonntag (formerly Veit-Simon) to Hermann.

24 May 1939

Dear Mutzi!

We were so pleased with your card. It is really wonderful that we will see each other before you go to Australia. Hopefully, in the next few days, you'll have time to come over to ours. It is terribly sad that Aunt Edith's condition is unchanged, but what can we expect with all the never-ending commotion.

On the one hand, the fact that Uncle Max is so busy is very good, but it must also be very sad for your mother because she feels better when he's around, doesn't she. Do you have any news from Rolf? Will you see him before your departure? Pass on my warm greetings to your parents when you write to them, okay?

For now, all the best and see you soon, your Ulla.
Many greetings and come over soon! Your Erich.

Hermann with his cousin Ulla and her daughter, Gabriele, at their home in Maida Vale.

*

The Gross Breeseners who were to board the SS *Strathallan* bound for Australia took the ferry from the Hook of Holland in Rotterdam across the North Sea to the port of Harwich, England. On the ferry's sundeck, rows of wooden day beds, deck chairs and timber benches held reclining passengers, their faces tilted to the sun, newspapers resting across their chests. Some sat up and penned letters, while others looked over the rails at the ocean.

Harwich was lined with shipping containers and old cranes. The Gross Breeseners boarded the train to London, each anticipating the bustling city. Alighting at Liverpool Street Station, they were met by the mess of the central London thoroughfare: double-decker buses plastered with advertisements, hundreds of motorcars grumbling and honking, swathes of pedestrians, cyclists and traffic controllers conducting the chaos from the centre of the road. Blue sky peeked through the grey as Hermann and the Gross Breeseners stood outside the station. A few of the students, Hermann included, had family with whom they could stay during these interim days. The rest secured lodgings at Bloomsbury House, the central refugee committee headquarters in London, from which thousands of Jewish refugees received help with their emigration out of Europe.

It was midafternoon at Tilbury Docks. The ship's bow towered 25 metres above the water, its body stretched 200 metres. Its name, *Strathallan*, was emblazoned in huge lettering at the bow.

Reaching high above the vessel was the mast, a tall, thin pole with a smaller one across it, strung up with rope like a cross. In the centre of the ship, the huge yellow chimney was already steaming, billowing greyish smoke high up into the equally grey clouds. Smaller tugboats and trawlers rocked lazily around the *Strathallan*, dwarfed by its magnitude. It was difficult to believe that, beneath the water's surface, the ship's body continued down even further; and yet its weight of more than 23,000 tonnes floated on the harbour quite still, only moving slightly with the undulations of the water, like a rowboat on a calm lake.

As departure time grew closer, more people descended upon the dock, armed with luggage, thick coats and scarves, possessions deemed essential to carry with them to new lives across the ocean. Children ran free along the wood-panelled boulevard; families embraced and said farewells; shipmen and crew carried out their duties. Moments of immense pain and emotion melded with other moments of ordinary life, the momentous and the mundane alongside one another, in the same place, at the same hour, beneath the same overcast sky.

The Gross Breeseners presented their tickets, along with their visa permits for Australia, to the ship's officials, and boarded the *Strathallan* alongside the many hundreds of other passengers. They found their cabins down below near steerage; Hermann was to share the tiny space with Bosi, a fellow Gross Breesener, and a Polish engineer they called The Pole. Jonny and Rudi shared another, while the others were dispersed to cabins with other passengers. Hermann tossed his trunk onto his small bed, took out his camera and a few postcards he'd purchased in a confectioner's shop in London, and made his way up to the main deck. The ship was not due to leave until 5pm, not for another hour. The Gross Breeseners met back up on the deck and wrote postcards home to family, or took photographs of their new transitory home—a kind of buoyant city completely foreign to anything they had ever seen.

Hermann wrote one postcard to his parents and one to his grandmother, detailing his time in London and his first impressions of the *Strathallan*. In detail, he described the unbelievable streets of London, the traffic, the hundreds of motorcars and bicycles pressed together for miles. He wrote of his hopes for them to one day join him in his new country once he completed his farm training and earned enough money to pay for their passage.

As the time for departure drew nearer, he finished writing and looked out over the railing of the main deck, leaning right over to touch the colourful paper bunting strung up along the rim to celebrate the commencement of the voyage. A band began playing on the lower deck and he craned his head over to hear it.

The moment had arrived.

Other passengers around him began to cheer and sing, in languages he could not pick. Down on the dock, people echoed the cheering and soon the moment was awash with sound and exhilaration. The ship's horn bellowed and was met with more cheering and applause. Gradually, almost imperceptibly, the ship began to pull away from the dock with the aid of a handful of tugboats. It moved slowly away from Tilbury as the fanfare continued.

'Doesn't it all look so tiny from up here!' remarked Jonny over the noise of the deck.

Hermann nodded, holding his camera up to his eye. 'They all look like ants,' he replied, and pointed down to the remaining people on the dock, shrinking in size with each passing second.

As the *Strathallan* started to gain pace through the Thames towards the sea, the Gross Breeseners fixed their gaze on the place they had just left. Before long, Tilbury was a faint blip in the distance and there was nothing in view but the leaden sky and its counterpart, the North Sea. Hermann breathed in the cool, salty air and stayed his focus on the journey ahead. In each of their minds was the song the Gross Breeseners had sung when they were all together at what felt like a lifetime ago:

And soon it will be true
that we stand by the sea
and think of the distant homeland;
for the little troop intensely prepares
to abandon the old grey stone walls.
Nothing keeps us anymore.
Overjoyed we'll leave shore;
soon our sails will flutter eastward.[31]

Days passed easily on board the *Strathallan*, and soon the only real markers of the passing time were the morning, afternoon and evening meals. For many on board, the previous few months or even years had seen a scarcity of food. Such pleasures that came with a delicious meal—superior cuts of meat, multiple courses and countless choices of dessert—

had for so long been figments of faraway desire, but were now presented on silver platters by well-dressed stewards. Every evening when the dinner gong rang at 7.30, Hermann and the other Gross Breeseners rushed to their cabins from wherever they were—usually the recreation deck—put on ties and fresh shirts, splashed water on their faces, combed their hair and raced back up to the dining hall. Their enthusiasm for the evening meals never diminished, because the meal itself, the act of sitting at the dining table with friends, evoked nostalgia of such rituals long abandoned.

The dining hall for the tourist class stretched across a whole floor and was lined with curtain-laced windows. Each table was dressed with a fresh white tablecloth and set with matching white plates and silver cutlery. On each plate was a menu card for the forthcoming meal of entree, main and dessert, a selection of which each passenger could choose according to their taste preference that day. Each passenger dressed well for dinnertime, as afterwards there was usually some form of entertainment: a band playing, passengers dancing and drinking well into the evening. Conversation filled the warm room, accompanied by a group of orchestral musicians in the corner.

The Gross Breesen group entered the impressive dining room and sat down at a long wooden table. At the vacant end sat a Polish family. Hermann sat next to the father.

'Good evening,' said Hermann, practising his English. The man remained silent, shaking his head. His scruffy dark hair was combed back and his faded white shirt buttoned tightly at the neck. The Polish man sat with his two children, a boy who looked about 12, and a girl who looked younger, maybe eight. His wife was silent and wore a silk scarf over her hair, a few soft dark curls falling around her face. She smiled at Hermann and the other Gross Breeseners as she held her daughter, nestled under her arm, too shy to look up.

'No English,' the man replied quietly, and motioned to himself and his family.

Hermann looked down at the menu card and felt for the family, who seemed lost with the indecipherable words.

'German?' Hermann asked the man.

'Ah!' he said, raising his eyebrows. 'A little,' he responded in German.

The steward came around to take their table's orders. Hermann read the menu to the man in German. He reached würstchen (sausages) and the man nodded. The man then recited the menu to his family in Polish, and Hermann ordered for the whole family in English, reciting each meal as the steward notated furiously with his pen and paper.[32] Hermann ordered the sausages for himself, too.

After dinner, when their bellies were full to bursting, some of the Gross Breeseners went out onto the promenade deck to smoke their pipes. Hermann went with them, despite his heavy eyelids. They huddled together, standing against the ship's railing, and looked out over the edge into the blackness. They could see nothing in front of them; they could only hear the roaring of the waves below and feel the cool wind as it whipped their cheeks and stole their tobacco smoke upwards into the night.

Later, when their conversation tired, the Gross Breeseners returned to their cabins. Hermann and Bosi crept quietly because The Pole was fast asleep in his bunk, snoring loudly with his mouth hanging open. The cabin captured all of the day's heat and it refused to ease. The hot air was stagnant in the small space, with no window for escape. Each bunk bed was equipped with its own small fan; passengers had to choose between the loud droning noise of the fans' little motors or the stale cabin heat. Hermann took off his jacket, shirt and pants, then got into his bunk and turned on the fan. Warm moving air was better than warm still air. He positioned his head right below the fan and closed his eyes. The fan almost drowned out The Pole's snores, but Hermann needn't have worried; before ten minutes passed, he was fast asleep himself.

The following day, Hermann and the other Gross Breeseners found a spot on the sports deck to enjoy the Mediterranean sunshine. Passengers lined the deck on beds with their eyes closed, faces shimmering in the heat. This kind of weather, blue skies and a warm breeze, made the ship's deck a passenger's paradise. Hermann found a place to sit and closed his eyes for a minute, wearing the warmth like a long robe. Then he pulled out the letter that had arrived for him from his parents and began to read.[33]

13 June 1939

Dear Mutzi,

Hopefully these lines find you healthy, and you have made it through the first days of your sea journey well …

Today, a long and very nice letter arrived from Erich and Ulla, in which they report about your visit. Erich is going to send the pictures he took of you. I am already looking forward to it.

We are, of course, very curious about what you will write to us. I just wish that you would send us a detailed report about all that you've experienced. How was the journey through the Channel? What did you do and see in London? How are the living conditions on the ship and so on? As you can imagine, we are interested in everything you experience and there is nothing in the world we care more about. However, you have to take your time and collect your thoughts in order to write a proper letter, which actually contains substance.

Now, on board you will have plenty of time; and you'll also get something out of meticulously putting your experiences to paper. Since we keep your letters, in the future, as you sit in the hall of your impressively furnished large estate, you can delight your wife and children by reading to them about your beginnings (provided that your loved ones understand German, or you have learned so much English that you can translate).

Hermann paused. The thought that his future family would be Australian and not German confounded him. He couldn't yet picture it, given that the land itself still mystified him.

Before I forget—for checking purposes, from now on I will number the letters so you can tell if you receive every single letter. So, if you don't throw my letters away, you could easily determine if a number is missing. You can do the same with the letters you send to us, but you have to take note which numbers have already been used.

I would like to take this opportunity to remark something. If you come into contact with such people who potentially could be helpful with advice and assistance, it is inappropriate to ask for favours from other people, whom you're trying to help. Otherwise, the person offering assistance could easily get a fright and think it is better not to start at all. So—every man for himself!

*Well—*chacon pout soi! *There's nothing interesting to report from here. I am fairly busy. Mutti is like always. Oma was here today, she will write to you herself. She's been here daily, because since last Thursday, Fräulein Hanna has been sick and bedridden ... Oma was very helpful and assisted the maid, who had to come, of course. On Saturday, Ruth and Etta*[34] *want to come over again for another tipple. Ruth has good prospects to leave. She's waiting for an affidavit for the USA, once she has it she can go to England until it's her turn. It is difficult to find something for Etta. Also, for the old ones, the chances are pretty bad ...*

It's turned two in the afternoon, office hours at the surgery are over and nothing's happened since yesterday evening. I will try to send the next letter via airmail to Port Said. Now a patient is shuffling in, after this I'll go buy a reply slip and then away with it.

Stay healthy, beloved Mutzi, and fondest greetings and kisses from, Mutti and Vati.

Kurt (a Gross Breesener) and Marianne (a fellow passenger), on board the SS Strathallan, *taken by Hermann Pollnow, 1939.*

Travelling on the same trajectory as the *Strathallan* was the SS *Slamat*, a Dutch ship that carried the second group of Gross Breeseners. The two groups were to join together on the *Strathallan* in Colombo for the remaining passage to Australia. For now, through the Mediterranean, the two ships and their passengers united at each port.

In Marseille, the *Slamat* docked alongside the *Strathallan*, so close that the Gross Breeseners could wave at each other from each ship's deck. They were briefly reunited for the afternoon while the ships were in port. After taking a tour of each ship, the group wedged into a taxi to visit the city sights.

Erich, who had for weeks admired the clothes of the men on

board the *Slamat*, those who dressed not just for utility but for style, had his mind set on purchasing a new jacket—one he could wear to the dining hall; long and white. He confided this wish to Hermann as they wandered the cobbled streets.

'Alright, we can keep a lookout for a shop,' Hermann said, conscious that it was already midafternoon and they were under strict instructions to be back at the ship by 4.30, because the *Slamat* left at 5 pm. Soon they came across a warehouse with men's jackets displayed in the front window. Erich slowed and peered through the glass. Convinced this was the place, he disappeared into the shop. Hermann stood outside and looked down at his watch with each passing minute. Finally, Erich stepped back outside empty-handed. The shop was much too expensive. He wanted to try one more store that he had spied further down the street.

'But the ship, Erich! We were supposed to be back at half past,' said Hermann.

'We'll make it back, I promise!' The boys traipsed back to the other shop and Erich disappeared again. It was just past 4.30. Hermann was riddled with worry. He knew the consequences of Erich missing his boarding call: he'd be stranded in France with no money for another ticket. The thought shot panic through him. The other Gross Breeseners were all back at the dock by then, and Hermann began to imagine the dire situation arising if they were trapped in Europe. He went into the shop to grab his friend, but he was nowhere to be seen. He must have gone into another shop without Hermann noticing. He paced the street, searching each shop for Erich, but he could not find him. He stared down the packed street. It was hopeless.

At 4.55, Hermann could wait no longer. He leaped into a taxi and it sped towards the dock. On the way back, he hoped he might spot Erich on the footpath, or that somehow Erich would make it back in time. But of this Hermann was not confident.

The taxi jolted to a halt and Hermann ran onto the dock, just in time to see the *Slamat* slowly pulling away from the quay. His heart sank for Erich, who had just missed his chance at escape.

'Hermann!'

Hermann whipped around to see Erich bolting down the dock, a new white dinner jacket under his arm. Erich's face turned pale as he saw the *Slamat*, at least 100 metres away by now.

Panicked, they looked around for anything that could get Erich to the ship. Hermann spotted a small motorboat with a man sitting in it, lazily reading a newspaper. The boys bolted to the boat and to the surprise of the man inside, pleaded with him to carry them out to the ship. The man chuckled and, seeing the desperate expression on young Erich's face, started the motor. Hermann jumped in the boat too, not wanting to miss the chance to see Erich clambering up the side of the *Slamat* on a rope ladder.

A crowd had gathered on the side deck of the *Slamat*. The other passengers watched incredulously as the motorboat sped towards the ship. The other Gross Breeseners on the *Slamat* clutched the railing and yelled at Erich and Hermann to hurry up. The motorboat pulled up to the side of the *Slamat*, where crew members slowly lowered a narrow metal stepladder. Hermann couldn't believe Erich's luck. Any later and there would have been no second chance at escape. Erich thanked the motorboat driver profusely in French and clapped Hermann on the back, beaming.

Erich boarding the SS Slamat, *taken by Hermann Pollnow, 1939.*

The SS Slamat, *taken by Hermann Pollnow from the SS* Strathallan *while anchored in Marseille, 1939.*

'See you in Colombo, Poscho!'

A ship steward stood on the stairs to help Erich onto the ship.

'You've got luck on your side, boy!' he said as Erich clambered onto the steps, still holding his brand-new jacket. Some of the onlooking passengers applauded as Erich made his way onto the *Slamat*.

'You'll get my bill for the boat!' Hermann yelled.

Erich grinned and waved, then disappeared onto the ship.

The ship sailed passed the Italian coast, often coming so close to the shore that, from the deck, passengers could see houses dotted along it. They passed by Greece and would soon be nearing Egypt. The night before the ship was to reach Port Said, Egypt, Hermann, Kurt and Guenther slept outside on the deck, on a row of lounge chairs, so they wouldn't miss the view coming into the port.

Above them, the sky was clear. They each looked up at the stars, millions of them, more stars than any of them had ever seen. The ocean mirrored the sky, vast and calm and indigo dark. The ship floated through this magnificent galaxy, quite far away, Hermann felt, from the rest of the world. Hermann shivered, though the wind blew soft and mild. He blinked away his tiredness, they all did, for hours, until the sky began to lighten ever so slightly. Small, rickety fishing boats appeared and soon, out of nothing, began a coastline. The boys got up and leaned over the railing, squinting through the early morning mist to the faint outline of Cairo.

The *Slamat* trailed closely behind them. Guenther and Hermann ran to the back of the ship to see if any of the others were on deck. Soon the two ships sailed side by side, headed for the port. Hermann spied Erich and Herko, another Gross Breesener, waving from the deck. The two ships reached Port Said at 5am and docked close enough that they could call out to each other.

'Ahoy!' Hermann yelled with all his might.

'Ahoy!' the Gross Breeseners on board the *Slamat* yelled back. The back and forth continued for another hour until the *Slamat* sailed off again. The *Strathallan* would follow a few hours later, headed down the Suez Canal.

28 June 1939

Dear Mutzi,

The day before yesterday your thick letter arrived from Port Said, which gave us great joy. Hopefully [letters] *no. 2 sent to Port Said and no. 3 sent to Bombay are with you. I also wrote to Marseille, didn't I? Did you receive the copies from Holland? It's worth confirming that you've received our mail …*

We don't get to experience much. Actually there is nothing going on, which is not a bad thing …

I just spoke to Aunt Anna on the phone, who sends warm greetings to you.

The tomcat is still cute, but completely outrageous. He

used to just catch our feet when they were sticking out from under the blanket; now he reaches under the blanket, which always wakes us up with a start. He is very nosy and always wants to see the patients when I'm consulting. After I'm seduced by his pleading into showing him, I sit him out in front of the door again, and he stays there and makes such a riot that I have to ask Hanna to take him away ...

This letter is your welcome to a new part of the world, one that will hopefully bring with it the fulfilment of your dreams and ours. We believe in you, and we don't think you will disappoint us. Since your birth, we have done everything we could for you. We hope you will repay us by becoming a diligent man, who will rise to the challenge of whatever position you are in and who will, with all your strength, meet the expectations of all the people who love you and have helped you on your path.

Remember what I said to you on your last trip to Berlin. You know that I am a man who knows life and people, and my advice is worth heeding. You are a reputable character, and we hope you will keep this quality your whole life. Beware of bad influences; without being suspicious, be careful in dealing with other people—in every relationship—if you don't know them very well. You don't always have to say everything that's on your mind, but you don't need to lie or pretend. So that's enough warnings for now. Stay healthy!

Mutti is sending you countless greetings and kisses, so too is your Vati.

In the quiet of evening, not one moment went by that Hermann's thoughts did not drift to the wellbeing of his parents in Berlin. Even on board the *Strathallan*, miles away from his old life, Hermann could not escape the reality of the danger encroaching on his parents, with worrying reports on the wireless and newspaper bulletins on board. He listened to stories of the danger he so narrowly escaped. Stretches of time passed with no word from them, and when he did receive a letter, it was clear that his father's words were measured. It seemed Max was careful not to reveal too much about Berlin home life, which, at that stage, on the cusp of war, was undoubtedly far more harrowing than his letters allowed Hermann to believe. Hermann knew that at this moment his parents joining him in Australia was an impossibility; he had experienced firsthand the exceedingly difficult process of securing permits to emigrate.

The Pollnows, by now, did not have enough money to buy a permit, nor the ship fare needed for a trip to the other side of the world. Max's income was a fraction of what it once was and Edith, due to the constant distress, grew more unwell each day. The Pollnows were trapped, but Hermann had a chance at life.

He would never take it for granted.

8

Inside the car, it is silent. We drive further down the South Coast, past roadworks, excavations and land clearing. If you focus on the horizon, you can glimpse the original beauty of the place—the green hills, the bushland—away from the levelled-out house plots and industrial main strip. It's hard to imagine the coast untouched by construction. Yet in the glint of sunlight through gum leaves and branches, the swift flourishes of birds beyond the telegraph poles, I see the remnants of the coast as it once was, before the soil was overturned to make roads.

We drive towards the hospital where Harry has been admitted again after another troubling night. We fear the time when Harry can no longer live at home is fast approaching. None of us know what this upheaval would mean for Harry, now that his mental and physical health seems to be dwindling after 100 years of fight. He needs round-the-clock care; he cannot be left alone. What if he falls? What if he forgets where he is?

The wind is up and clouds form over the glaring midday sun, accumulating behind the faded, yellow-brick building. We reach the ward with relative ease, despite the protest from a NSW Health official, who is adamant that only one visitor per patient is allowed due to Covid. A hospital security guard, a woman with thick curly hair and a heavy tread, murmurs to my mother that on occasion, depending on the patient, more than one visitor can sneak through. The official is an older woman with her face covered by a blue surgical mask. At first, she states the one-person-per-patient rule firmly.

'Please,' says Mum. 'We've driven from Sydney. My dad's 100 years old and he doesn't know what the hell's going on.'

The official sighs.

'I give up,' she exclaims, and waves us towards the ward entrance.

We turn into Harry's room and I have to take a moment to recognise him. He looks so different from when I saw him last, smaller maybe, some of the colour drained from his face. He sleeps with his mouth half open and his hands clasped together over his chest. The nurse tells us he didn't get much sleep last night so she let him sleep all morning. He wears a white singlet that sits unevenly over his chest. The skin over his forearms is scabbed and bruised, something I have grown used to seeing, but the marks are no less unnerving. He looks like he's been in a fight. The skin across his neck is sunken and his thinning grey eyebrows are tilted downwards at their far corners.

'Let's not wake him up,' Mum whispers, and I nod.

The room is like any other hospital room. They all share that sterilised quality, a poor simulation of home. Window, curtains, chairs, desk, bed, TV, toilet. The floors are speckled blue linoleum and the bed looks more like a mechanical contraption. It's covered in wires and headed by a flashing switchboard. Mum immediately starts tidying the tray table and pulls a plastic chair towards the bed, then sits down and retrieves the newspaper crossword from her handbag. I take the other chair near the window. Mum glances at Harry every few seconds. We watch his chest as it rises and falls, soft swells. I turn on the television and flick through the muted channels. I pause on a news report about the family from Biloela, Queensland, being detained on Christmas Island, despite arriving in Australia as legal asylum seekers.[35]

Harry wakes shortly after we settle. He blinks slowly, casts his gaze over the room.

'Hi, Dad.' Mum leans into his line of vision and catches his eye. The hearing aid in his right ear tunes her words. I listen to the soft, high-pitched whistling of that tiny machine at work.

'Julia,' he gurgles, the word stuck in his throat.

'Tess, can you get his drink?' Mum motions to the plastic mug on his tray table. It's three-quarters full of fluoro-green Staminade. I pass it to Mum, who lifts it to his mouth. He takes two small sips and coughs.

'Thank you,' he murmurs in the voice I know. I exhale with relief.

He looks around the room as if for the first time, total unfamiliarity. I follow his gaze across the chalky paper curtain, a partition between us and the corridor. On the other side of the room a small window looks out to the carpark. I can see our car, parked beneath a tinder-dry gumtree. On Harry's tray table is a stack of small photo albums, a half-eaten banana, yesterday's newspaper and a folded piece of paper on which someone has written: 'Hello! You are in hospital. You are being looked after. You have lost your memory!'

Mum and I watch him, waiting for any sign that he knows where he is or what is happening. He reaches for the tubular plastic bottle next to him with a pained expression.

'I'll get the nurse,' says Mum. She calls down the corridor.

Mum and I step outside as two masked nurses march into the room and close the door.

'Are you alright?' Mum asks me.

'Yeah, I'm okay.'

Really, though, I'm shaken by Harry's visible deterioration. Mum peeks her head inside the room.

'Can you get him up and into the chair?' she asks the nurses.

A pause.

'Thanks.'

While we wait, I wander down the hospital corridor. The nurses' station is right outside Harry's room. It is virtually deserted except for one woman who is on the phone, facing away from me. The rest are on their feet; there must be a team of ten or so on this floor alone. I can't help but peer into the rooms along the corridor. Most of them are shared, each hospital bed partitioned off by a paper curtain. Every patient I can see is old. Most look calm lying in their beds. I wander further, deeper down the ward. One patient is up and walking around by herself, holding on to an orange plush toy, a lion. I smile as I pass her. She is shorter than me, wrinkled and grey-skinned. Her hair comes to her shoulders, thins at her crown and falls over her face in limp strings.

'Can I have a hug?' she asks me.

I do not know what to reply, and I remember that she can't see my smile beneath my mask. A younger woman—her daughter,

I guess—runs up beside her and holds her arm. She nods at me and turns the woman around, back towards her room.

I look back at Mum, who is now on the phone outside Harry's room. One hand holds her phone up to her ear and one is blocking the other. The thrum of medical equipment, the continuous beeping and patient cries are relentless, yet the employees here move so swiftly and purposefully. Two unused wheelchairs sit waiting at the end of the corridor, along with other disused machines I don't recognise. I can only guess at their use. I sit in one of the wheelchairs, feel its stretched leather arms under my own and put my feet on its two metal footrests that hover just above the floor. I put my hands over each wheel and slowly rock myself back and forth. I am suddenly conscious of the agency I have over my own body. It's a new thought, one I do not often register or appreciate.

Another patient hobbles down the corridor, a woman holding a small suitcase in one hand and a green Woolies bag in the other. It looks like she's going somewhere. Maybe she is discharged? She is frail and walks slowly with a hunch. I notice she is still wearing her hospital gown and no shoes. She approaches the nurses' station and says something to the woman at reception. I cannot hear the conversation. She speaks again, more adamantly, pointing to the exit, two large glass doors that require a staff swipe to open. One of the nurses goes to her side and holds the woman under her right arm, takes the green bag out of her hand and carries it. Then she gently guides her back to one of the rooms with the paper partition curtains.

Mum is off the phone and has her head inside Harry's room. I see the door widen; the light bleeds into the corridor and the two nurses march out. They veer off into another room two doors down from Harry.

When I re-enter Harry's room I see, as instructed, he is sitting up in the chair by the window, dressed in tracksuit pants and a checked collared shirt, which I recognise from another time. Some colour has returned to his face. It's odd to see him dressed as he would be at home, but in this room. Mum has brought the wheeled table close to him and he is regarding its contents. She sits opposite, watching him. As I come closer he looks up and smiles, I suspect more out of politeness than actual recognition.

'Hi, Harry, how are you?' I take off my mask, kiss him on the cheek and squeeze his forearm. His eyes are unfocused, still groggy from sleep.

'Not bad,' he replies. He looks out the window. '*Windisch*,' he says and points outside. It's true: a gust has picked up and is tousling the trees that line the carpark outside.

'Yes, quite windy today,' says Mum. She can guess at that word.

Another masked nurse enters with a trolley trailed by a warm, savoury smell.

'Lunch,' she says. She takes out a tray and places it on the table. I grab the albums and put them on the windowsill. I notice an envelope sitting on Harry's bedside table, labelled *Harry's 100th Birthday Cards*.

'There you are, Dr Peters,' she says. They've written *Dr Peters* on his patient board.

'He can't understand you through the mask,' says Mum. 'He has to lip-read.'

The nurse nods and waves at Harry, who waves vacantly back.

I peel the plastic lid off Harry's lunch. Chicken breast with gravy, mashed potato and green vegetables. I take the knife and fork and begin cutting up the chicken into bite-sized pieces. I load a piece of chicken and a small broccoli floret onto the fork and guide it into his open mouth. I put the fork down and he resumes; he can feed himself.

'*Wo sind die Schützen*?'

Mum looks at me, as if I understand. I shrug.

'English, Dad, speak English. What are you saying?'

'*Schützen*,' he says again, then he holds up his hands, one pulled back and pointed behind his ear, the other out in front and curved, cradling the barrel of an invisible gun. He makes a *pop* sound with his lips.

'*Schützen*.'

Pop, pop, pop.

Mum looks at me again. I pull out my phone and quickly look for the Google translation.

'Shooters,' I murmur.

Harry is looking out the window again, armed with his invisible weapon. *Pop, pop, pop*.

'It's okay, Dad. There are no shooters. You are safe here.'

'Am I?'

'Yes. Come on, eat your lunch.'

He gets about a quarter of the way through his meal then motions it away with his hands.

'Enough,' he says.

The three of us recede into our respective quiet places, in our chairs looking out to the carpark—me, down at the floor. I trace the cords that snake around Harry's bed and try to match them to their origin on the big switchboard. No-one knows how long he will stay here. I want to believe that because of his weary brain he doesn't quite know what is happening; he hasn't yet guessed that he may not be going home, ever. We don't know either, really. The doctors said that the infection will reoccur, that he will never be rid of it, that they could keep treating it with antibiotics but eventually, after that stops, it will come back again. They said that this infection will most likely be what kills him.

'Who lives here?' he asks after a time.

'No-one, Dad. You are staying here for a while until you are well enough to go home.'

'What's wrong with me?'

'You have an infection. But you are getting better. The doctors here are very good.'

'Are they?'

'Yes.'

Photo albums are a small miracle in this room, otherwise completely devoid of stimulation or distraction. I slowly flip through one in front of him, as if I am telling a story to a child, careful to point out each detail. My eyes flick to his every few moments, to see if he feels any familiarity. I pause on one in black and white taken at Mount Kosciuszko. He's in his racing gear posing next to another man I don't recognise. In the background, the mountains of the main range are covered in, and the gumtree branches are weighed down by snow.

'*Schnee!*' he says.

'Do you remember him?' I ask, pointing to the other man.

'Ja, John.'

I flip the photo after a few more moments.

A warden enters the room, a wave of fresh energy. When he enters, he flicks his mask off one ear so it hangs, revealing a tanned face wrinkled with a smile. His hair is blond but greying and is swept back off his face.

'How are you, Dr Peters?' he asks, and I can tell he has spoken with him before from the way he projects and annunciates each word.

'Very well, thanks,' Harry replies warmly.

The warden turns to Mum.

'My name's Mick,' he says. 'I've been around the last few days checking in on Harry. I just wanted to pop in and tell you that your father is a real legend. I've been in this industry 30 years, and there's no-one who doesn't know Dr Harry Peters.'

I glance at Mum, who I can tell is holding back tears.

'It's an honour to be looking after him,' says Mick. 'Anyway, just thought I'd tell you.'

'Thank you,' I say, and Mum thanks him as well.

Mick touches Harry on the shoulder. 'You'll let me know if you need anything, okay, Dr Peters?'

'Sure,' says Harry.

We stay in the room well into the afternoon until the sun disappears, leaving in its wake a sky tinged orange. I feel in a daze, my mind dampened by today's inertia, sitting still but burning through nervous energy. I wonder when we might leave; I know Mum and I are both dreading it because it means Harry will be alone.

'You take such good care of me,' says Harry, and he begins to weep. 'Please don't leave me. Don't leave me, Mutti.'

'Don't cry, Dad,' says Mum, as she moves to sit by him.

'Don't cry, it's alright.'

'Where are my parents?' he weeps.

Neither Mum nor I say anything.

'Mutti!' he cries. 'Where is Mutti?'

'It's okay, Dad. We're here.'

'I want to go home,' he wails, and I feel it in my stomach.

'You can't go home, Dad. You have to stay here until you're better.'

A nurse enters the room with a tray of clear plastic cups filled with different-coloured pills. She takes one and places it on Harry's tray table. Mum grabs it.

'Here, Dad, take this.'

'No!' he says, with vitriol.

'Take it, Dad, it will make you feel better.'

'I want to go home!'

After a while, maybe ten minutes, he relents and takes the pill. I'm not sure what it is—some kind of relaxant, probably, to help him into sleep. To numb him. The nights are not easy, I recall the nurse telling us at the start of the day. We sit with him at his bedside, as his weeping dims but persists in quiet, meek exhales. There's nothing more we can do, I keep telling myself. Mum whispers we should go, undetected by his hearing aid. As he lulls into sleep, we gather our things and leave. I try not to think about him waking, which he will, to find himself alone in a strange room.

'There's nothing more we can do,' Mum says, as we walk down the corridor towards the exit.

'I know,' I say. 'It's just hard.'

Guilt descends as we get in the car and reverse away from

the hospital. But there is nothing to be done about it, at least not tonight. He cannot go home.

The air is cool. Traces of sun are still on the far horizon, a small curve of light as it makes its way downwards. I will be glad when this day ends. On the drive home, I feel a pang of grief: for Harry, for Mum, for the time somewhere in the future when I will have to hold the hand of my own parent as the world around them becomes unrecognisable.

A feeling of shared anticipation encircled the Gross Breeseners as they approached their new home country. They had spent so many hours talking about their plans, how their new lives might take shape, the prospect of continuing on with their youthful ambitions while so many others were still in Germany trying to leave. The Gross Breeseners were family, as they were at the farm, then inside Buchenwald, then at Nieuwesluis. Nearing ever closer to Australia, the reality of their impending separation grew inside each of them, a familiar feeling of unease. Their fates lay beyond their grasp, in the hands of organisations, committees and wealthy guarantors.

Strangers.

The *Strathallan* neared the port of Melbourne on the evening of 16 July 1939. Having already docked at Fremantle, Western Australia, the first stop in their new country, the Gross Breeseners were now acquainted with some of the more obvious peculiarities of Australian culture. Crossing the street, they had to have their wits about them, because in this country people drove on the other side of the road. Australians spoke quickly, at times indecipherably, and on more than one occasion Hermann had been called a 'bloody reffo!'—a term many European immigrants would learn to wear.

The Australian Jewish Welfare Society, founded in 1936, was the organisational body that oversaw the influx of German-Jewish immigrants into Australia. The Welfare Society secured employment, found accommodation and provided what assistance it could to the refugees in their new country. Australia's response to Jewish immigration at this time, on the cusp of war, was mixed. The Sydney and Melbourne Jewish communities, established long before, were already assimilated into Australian society, and were not always welcoming to their European counterparts. The refugees stood out: they spoke different languages, they dressed in long trench coats, they looked foreign, they moved in close-knit groups, and many brought with them an air of cultural and intellectual sophistication bred in Europe's metropolitan upper middle class that was not appreciated in the relatively barren cultural landscapes of Australian cities.

The threat of anti-Semitism was rife in Australia too, and it was the general position of society that traces of foreignness should be erased. Paranoia about German spies and foreign infiltration neared its peak with this wave of refugees. So it was that Australia's reception of German-Jewish refugees, despite the knowledge of Nazi persecution, imprisonment in camps and disintegration of their human rights, was not the warm welcome many had expected.

At the Welfare Society office on Collins Street in Melbourne, Hermann stood in a small room with the others and waited for

ADELAIDE: SATURDAY, JULY 22, 1939.

Let's Get The Best Refugees

ALLEGATIONS that many of the refugees entering Australia are undesirable have been made by prominent men recently. Mr. Holden, M.L.C., said on his return from abroad that he was greatly concerned about the type receiving permits from Canberra; many refugees were totally unsuitable and had neither money nor a job to come to. Mr. Cowan, a fellow-M.L.C., spoke even more strongly in Parliament. He said that Australia wanted the right kind of settler with capital to swell her population, but instead she was getting a most undesirable type, who would be a menace to society and a burden to the taxpayer.

These criticisms follow closely on the statement by Sir Frank Clarke, of Victoria, that "slinking, rat-faced aliens with 20-in. chests were working in Melbourne factories and threatening social standards." This broadside was investigated by Commonwealth officers, who said they could not find one instance of the alleged back-yard factories, and also that aliens who had recently entered the Commonwealth were of good physique.

Nevertheless, it is inconceivable that there should not be some truth in these and other criticisms. Everyone knows that Australia is getting many splendid refugees who will greatly benefit the land of their adoption—the eight young Hitler-fearing men who went to Kuitpo Colony this week appeared to be in this class—but at the same time too many undesirables seem to be sneaking in.

Fortunately, something is being done to select migrants more carefully. The Federal Government has realised that it is impossible to make the selection satisfactorily in Australia, from letters written by would-be migrants, and has appointed an officer at Australia House, London, to interview applicants for permits.

He has only a small office, with a frosted window on the Aldwych frontage of the House bearing the words "Commonwealth of Australia. Alien Migration and Refugees. Inquire Within"; but he is bearing an enormous responsibility. He is the keeper of the gate, admitting this one and turning that one away lamenting. To some degree the fashioning of Australia's future is in his hands.

Yet, when Mr. Holden left England, this official's term had only three months to run, and Mr. Holden was told that it was not intended to replace him. Australia will be making a blunder if he is not replaced. Not only should the office be retained, but additional officials should be appointed so that Australia will have an adequate staff in London to interview and select refugees.

Every thinking Australian agrees that this country needs more people, and there are so many refugees at present that we can afford to pick and choose the 15,000 we are admitting over three years. England has welcomed Sigmund Freud, and America is giving refuge to such outstanding men as Einstein and Thomas Mann. Brains like these may not be available for Australia, but there is plenty of other good material with which we can build up our national life. Let's see that we get it.

Excerpt from The Mail *(Adelaide), Saturday 22 July 1939.*[36]

the committee to make its decision about which six refugees were to stay behind and which were to go on to Sydney. There was no official welcome, no acknowledgement of the monumental journey on which they had just embarked. There was little sympathy for these teenagers who had left behind everything. They were refugees now. They stood in a line and a committee member, without so much as a second glance, changed their names.

'Hermann Pollnow,' said the man. 'Your name is now Harry Peters.'

Harry Peters.

Hermann, now Harry, murmured his new name a few times to get his tongue around it. His accent was thick; it sounded nothing like how the committee man said it. Harry wondered what his parents would think of the name change. Max was worried enough about the prospect of changing his middle name to Israel! Now the names of both his grandfathers, Hermann and Ludwig, and his last name, Pollnow, the name that marked centuries of history in Germany, were erased.

Your name is now Harry Peters.

The Welfare Society informed the refugees that outside, where they would be living in the cities and in the country, the Australian people were hostile towards foreigners. Not much reasoning was given for this, and Harry couldn't think of why this would be. Had the Australian people not heard of the atrocities occurring in Europe? It seemed that paranoia towards those who were different was common across borders. This was why, at the close of the meeting, each Gross Breesener left with a British name, with their trench coats altered to suit the British style, and with the strict instruction to not congregate in big groups and to never utter a word of German in public.

Harry and five other boys—Frank J., James, Frank S., George and Fred—were selected to stay behind while the rest of the group was to travel on to Sydney.[37] It was an unexpected change of plans. While they would have all liked to stay together, Harry was happy to finally have a confirmed destination: a trainee agricultural farm called Kuitpo Colony in South Australia. They were told it wasn't too far away from Adelaide. It was run by the Methodist Church and the colony's founder, Reverend Samuel Forsyth.

*

We came here in 1939. In June or July 1939. We landed in Melbourne and came off the boat, six of us, and went to the Jewish Welfare Society on Collins Street in Melbourne. The first thing they did was change our names. That was done in a rather offhand manner. We were lined up and they said, 'What's your name?' I said, 'Hermann Pollnow'. They replied, 'H.P., Harry Peters. What's your name? Günther Stranz. G.S., George Strong. Your name? Franz Danzinger. F.D., Fred Danby', and so on. That was done without asking whether we liked to or not.

We were taught not to shake hands, that was un-British or un-English, and not to put our feet together, not to wear long raincoats and so forth. We were then, the six of us, told that they would send us back to Adelaide, to the central mission, which was a Christian religious organisation, central Methodist, to learn Australian farming.

We went back to Adelaide and then to Kuitpo Colony, which was a colony about 60 kilometres south of Adelaide. It was a camp where they rehabilitated ex-prisoners before they returned to civil life. We were accommodated there in a railway carriage, which was where we had to sleep in raincoats because it was raining through. They allotted an ex-prisoner who was our cook, who was quite a nice fellow. And our farming experience existed in getting up at six and going into the bush, cutting down trees. We became quite expert tree cutters, or lumberjacks. We were paid five shillings a week, which was enough to buy stamps and a packet of cigarettes.

*

The Kuitpo Forest is a plantation in the Adelaide Hills, where Californian pine trees were planted on the grounds of native ones. The pine trees grow tall and very thin, uniform in their measured distances, which gives the impression that the forest is hollow. As opposed to the thick bushland skirting the forest, land not yet cleared, these trees were grown for the sole purpose of being cut down. Kuitpo was named after the Indigenous word for 'reeds', as in those along Blackfellows Creek nearby. The plantation stretches for kilometres; the bordering native bushland creeps closer to the rows of pines as they grow in tiny increments with each passing second. The introduced trees stand out from the scraggly grey gums and earthy foliage that rages with the wind; instead, they are straight as nails and silent.

Owing to the hardships of the Great Depression, Methodist Reverend Samuel Forsyth sought to aid single men left unemployed and destitute. He wanted to build a colony where men could earn their keep by learning skills on the land. In 1930, Forsyth and the first six colonists looked upon the dense forest and began hacking it back, clearing the land to make room to build their lodgings. Since those early days, the colony expanded to accommodate hundreds of men, cattle, sheep, poultry and horses. The colony produced its own meat, vegetables, bread and milk, and by the time Harry and the others arrived, Kuitpo Colony was almost entirely self-sustaining.

It was the depths of winter when Harry arrived. In Europe, life was built for the cold; here the cold was relentless, an undefeatable enemy. Fog encroached on every aspect of the road, so he could see nothing of his surroundings as they drove up to Kuitpo. When he got out of the bus and trudged up to the main building skirted by gumtrees, all he could think was that it was so different from anything he had imagined. The smell of recent rain on the eucalypts was strange. The dense bushland, the browns and greys, were nothing like the forests of Germany.

They were shown around the colony, the kitchen and dining hall, shower and washroom stalls and, finally, their lodgings in what was known in the colony as 'Railway Town': a line of discarded railway carriages that were used as accommodation for the workers. The refugees were allotted a carriage, repurposed with beds, drawers and a small table. Harry looked around the cabin, at the gaps between the windows and walls, the cracks in the roof, the floor that was already damp in places. It was colder in the carriage than outside, and he wondered what they were to do at night, when it got even colder and the rain pummelled the already sinking roof.

Harry did not know what exactly he imagined when he envisioned his new home, but it certainly was not this.

They were each given working clothes, an overcoat, a pair of stout boots, three woollen blankets, a bush rug, a towel and a pillowcase.[38] They were told to be grateful; there was a long list of Australian men desperate for a place here at Kuitpo.

The refugees did not have much to do with the Australian workers. They kept to themselves, still children compared to the burly and seasoned Kuitpo men. They were also unprepared for the icy nights of a South Australian winter. The brochures they were given had depicted bustling cities, magnificent architecture and a bridge on the edge of a shimmering, sunny harbour.

The reality of their first experience in Australia was quite different; so different it might have been another country altogether. Here, the bush was harsh, like nothing they had seen in Europe. The native trees looked haggard and unruly, the branches curled and splayed outwards with faded leaves hanging off them in bunches, limp before the sunlight and ferocious in the wind.

At home in Berlin, there was so much between Harry and the winter night: coal-fire heating, thick blankets and hearty meals. Here, there was nothing between the boys and the elements except an old layer of decaying metal. This was the promise of shelter and a new life in agriculture they had spent so many months dreaming about. Harry knew there were plenty who were in far worse circumstances, but as he lay awake and waited for morning, he could not help but long for the comforts of home he'd taken for granted.

The rain finally ceased as morning leaked into the carriage, first through the cracks in the walls, then through the frosted windows. Harry, wrapped in his overcoat, rose as the weak light drew silhouettes over his fellows sharing the carriage. They began work at 6am; it can't have been much earlier than that. As he got up, the others stirred.

'It's as cold as death in here!' said George. 'A few times in the night I thought my lungs were going to freeze through.'

The others agreed, still groggy with sleep.

'It's not right, making us live in this piece of junk.'

Harry pulled on his boots and stumbled out into the morning. From the carriage, he watched as the other men marched from their huts to the dining hall. Some stole a glance at him, one of the 'reffos'. The only Australian man the refugees had real contact with was their chef, an ex-prisoner, who cooked their morning and evening meals. Harry did not mind this divide; it was wise to keep a close-knit group, to stay together and not rouse attention. His father had instructed him to work hard above all else, so that is what he did.

They set off into the forest early, before the sun. By 7am the workmen were perspiring despite the morning frost, and the cracking of felled trees echoed through the otherwise quiet bushland. Harry knew this work; by now manual labour and farming was second nature. Their task was to begin clearing a new area, take to the trees with their axes, hack them to size and haul them into piles for firewood and the pottery oven. Harry listened to the Australian men in his work group, their fast, indecipherable English. They seemed indifferent to Harry and the other young refugees, and while none were outwardly hostile, none were too friendly, either. The group dispersed into the trees in pairs. They hacked into the trunks with saws and axes, heaving left and right as if fighting each other. Harry felt each blow in his arms and torso until it became rhythmic. Before long, he dropped his axe and stepped backwards as the tall narrow trunk and mass of spindly branches swung to the ground. The edges of the stump began to bleed.

'Looks like you lads have done this before!' one of the Australian men remarked, as he watched the refugees at work.

With as much confidence as he could muster, Harry smiled and nodded. 'Once or twice,' he said.

The Australian man nodded approvingly.

The days passed in this way. Once again, Harry's muscles

grew used to the gruelling labour of farm work. The nights, though, he never grew used to. Sleeping in the leaky carriage troubled Harry, not only because it provided little more comfort than sleeping in the open forest, but because none of the boys were given any indication of when their situation might change. Each day shivered into night, and night into morning. He wrote to his parents, not to worry them but to express his surprise at the place where he found himself. Harry knew he should be grateful that he was here and not back at that place he had so narrowly escaped; he knew this would be his father's response. He thought of his peers and friends back in Germany who had no chance at emigration and felt guilty for wanting an end to this immediate discomfort when those left behind faced far worse. Hard work helped silence his mind and made it a little easier to ignore the feeling of despair, agonising, heavy despair, at all that had been unjustly taken from him. Harry missed it all: his bedroom and Jonny the cat clawing his ankles, his Oma's roast chicken, cycling through the Tiergarten, knowing the city streets like the veins of his palm, old friends and family with whom he could speak freely, the ease of German on his tongue. He longed for the time, years ago, when life was unimpeded by the fear that everything could be gone tomorrow.

9

The decision to move Harry into a nursing home ends months of painful deliberation. With this a new phase begins, one not entirely different from the last few months, marred with anxiety and guilt and grief. Moving a loved one away from the place they know, especially when they have as loose a grip on reality as Harry does now, is heartbreaking. We are fortunate to be able to move him to a place like this, with a garden and a balcony and big windows in every room. Still, the closeness of death is inescapable. The air in here is heavy and cold. Every so often a resident screams from inside their bedroom; relatives weep in stiff armchairs in the communal lounge room. The pandemic restrictions mean we stagger our visits. One family member comes to see him every day of the week; my day is Thursday.

It's hard to say whether Harry's swift fall into dementia is due to the move or if it would have happened inevitably at his age. Probably a bit of both, I think. He is nearly never alone, except for late at night when he apparently wanders the corridors looking for his family. The nurses tell us that he is always looking for either Lynn or his parents. We are told that many of the residents are Holocaust survivors and the staff are equipped to deal with that sort of trauma. I wonder exactly what they're equipped with, how they're trained. What do the nurses do if a resident believes them to be Nazis and wails with fear at the sight of their uniforms? Or if, despite their incapacity, a resident spits and throws punches with shaking joints because they believe in that moment they're being forced into a covered truck?

Outside, the summer sun flares; I can see it radiate off the double-glazed windows. The windows are tinted so the light and warmth do not reach the room unless they're opened. Even then, the windows can only open a fraction. Today, they are firmly shut and the air inside is cold enough that I reach for my jumper and pull it on. I sit slouched in the armchair next to the bed and look around the room. I feel as if I know each corner of it by heart; I've sat in this very spot next to Harry's bed every week since he moved here in November. The room is identical to the ones on either side and the ones across the corridor, except for a few touches of home: a Japanese painting; the Star of David ornament, which once hung above Harry's armchair in Kiama; framed photos of family members; and the stacks of photo albums, his crucial connectors to reality. There are two cupboards for clothes, a small table-and-chair setting, a mini fridge, a bedside table, a television mounted on the wall, the armchair I'm sitting on and a bay window, where you can sit and look out to the serviced retirement units in the next complex over. The floors are pale blue, like you'd find in a hospital room, and the bathroom is similarly fitted out like a hospital, always with the faint scent of urine and disinfectant. The bed, which Harry rests in now, is the main feature of the room. All other furniture is built around the bed, the nucleus of this final stage.

Resting, sleeping, waiting.

Harry's lunch, now stone cold, sits on the wheelie tray table. He didn't touch his lunch, and only ate a few bits of his breakfast, the nurse told me as I arrived. He does not like the food here, so we bring in food he likes: ham, cheese, pickles, mustard, pumpernickel and vanilla ice cream.

He stirs. I smile at him, and he gives me a vague smile back. I'm not sure if he knows who I am, but I think he can register that I am someone in the family. I put down my laptop and turn the armchair closer to him. He is looking around the room with a blank expression. Many years have passed since he resigned himself to not knowing exactly where he is at any given time. He recognises people, and those places locked in photographs.

'Hi, Harry, did you have a nice rest?'

He nods.

'Would you like to get up now and go and sit in the sun for a while? It's a lovely day,' I say, trying not to sound like I'm speaking to a toddler.

'Yes, okay,' he says.

I press the button for a nurse to come and help change his clothes, and I get him a glass of juice. I hold it up to his lips and he takes a few gulps, then waves it away. The nurses arrive. At first Harry protests. I stand next to him and reassure him that they are here to help, that they are very nice and will not hurt him. Eventually he relaxes and allows the nurses to help him into trackpants, a singlet and collared shirt. Then one helps him to the bathroom and he brushes his teeth.

'Would you like him in the wheelchair?' one asks me.

'Yes, thanks. We'll go out to the courtyard, I think.'

'That's good. He hasn't been out of bed today,' says the nurse.

I nod and swallow the lump in my throat. I grab his straw sunhat and sunglasses from the bay window. They rest next to the small collection of exercise books the carers use to monitor Harry's moods and actions during their shifts. I place the hat and sunglasses on his lap, and wheel him slowly out of his room and into the corridor.

Outside each room along the corridor is a glass cabinet in which families of residents can place photos that might be recognisable to their loved one in case they get lost and need to find their way back to their room. Nurses nod their heads at me and smile. Other families of residents hurry past, preoccupied with their own issues.

I notice the room a few doors up from Harry's is getting emptied out by staff. Only a few weeks ago, when I was hovering in the corridor while Harry was going to the bathroom, I heard a voice crying out for help from that now-empty room. I walked towards the voice and found a man, whose name I never learned, clinging to the doorframe with shaking legs.

'Please help,' he said to me. 'I need to use the toilet.'

I went and pressed his nurse button for him, but nobody came.

'I'll go and find someone,' I said, and walked up and down the corridor until I found a nurse.

'Please, can you help the man down there?' I pointed down the corridor. 'He needs the toilet. His button has been pressed.'

'Okay, I'll be there in a minute,' she said, obviously distracted.

I walked back down the corridor to the man.

'Someone's coming now,' I said, and his face softened.

'Thank you,' he said.

I looked more closely at his face, wrinkled and shrunken, and saw a deep cratered scar on his left cheek.

'I've got another one here,' he said, pointing to his stomach.

I blinked, embarrassed that he caught me staring.

'Bullets, both of them,' he said.

'Wow,' I said. 'From when?'

'The war,' he said. 'Second one.'

The nurse I spoke to walked down the corridor towards us, wheeling a huge white contraption with a harness hanging from it, accompanied by two other nurses.

'All this for a pee,' he said, and I smiled, not knowing what to say.

Now the man's room is dark and empty, and a younger man of about 50 leaves it, carrying a pile of folded clothes with a few books perched on top.

We keep walking towards the lifts. I turn to look at an old woman sitting by herself in the lounge area to the right, where visitors and residents congregate. She is sitting still and staring out at nothing. She has been sitting there in that exact spot every time I visit. Next to the lift are two armchairs with a glass side table in the middle and a large bouquet of bird of paradise fronds sitting on it, next to a box of tissues. We hover at the lift next to another woman hunched over her cane. The lift bell sings, opening to floor-to-ceiling mirrors. I look at mine and Harry's reflection. He is alert, looking at me and then at the woman with the cane who has entered as well. I feverishly hope that he doesn't blurt out anything inappropriate due to his dementia, as he has been known to do on occasion.

To my immense relief, he looks at the woman and says,

'Hello, good day.'

She smiles and says, 'Good day', in reply.

Harry and I get out on level three, and I wheel him past the cafe out to the courtyard. The midafternoon sun beams off the paved ground. There's not a single cloud in the sky and the late January haze clings to everything: every flower, every tree, every pavement tile. While I nearly shudder from the intense heat, Harry sighs with delight.

'Oh, I love the sun,' he says, lifting his face upwards. 'Sehr schön!'

I wheel him to his favourite spot by the fishpond, drag a chair over and sit next to him. He is focused on the goldfish swimming in their raised concrete pond, darting beneath lily pads that to me look like plastic.

'It would get hot for them, in there,' he says. 'They go under there for shade.' He points to the group of about six fish as they disappear beneath the lily pads. Around us are other residents with their visitors. On the far side of the courtyard is one old man, wheeled out by a nurse and left alone, basking in the sun. I look at Harry, who is looking vacantly at the pond with his head tilted down slightly. I feel as though I need to draw him out of his present mind to somewhere more recognisable.

'Hey, Harry.' He looks at me. 'Do you remember the story of the white dinner jacket? With Eric?'

He pauses, thinking.

'Well, he wanted a white ... suit. And we found him, you know, a shop ...' he trails off.

'And did you have to rush back to the ship?'

He chuckles.

'Yes. He got a bit of a talking to.'

'What sort of things did you do on the ship?'

'Not much. Just walked around, looked overboard. *Strathallan*. It was a big ship.'

'Do you remember anything about the people who were on the ship with you?'

'No. Didn't know anybody much.'

I can tell he's trying to offer something more, but I don't want to push him.

'Do you remember what it was like coming into Australia?'

'Well, we were all quite pleased to land ... seeing different people. I think we started from Germany ...'

'You got on the ship at Tilbury Docks in London,' I say.

'Oh, yeah.'

'Tilbury Docks,' I repeat a bit louder.

He nods and gazes at the fishpond. 'It was a big ship.'

'Do you remember arriving in Australia?'

'In Australia ...'

'Do you remember what it was like when you got off the ship?'

'No.'

We sit for a while. Harry alternates between dozing and watching the fish.

'Harry, do you remember Kuitpo Colony?'

'Kuitpo ...'

'You worked there for a while, as a lumberjack. Chopping down trees.'

'Oh, yeah, I remember that. The man who worked there was Mr Bondy.'

'I think Bondy worked at Gross Breesen, didn't he?'

'Yes, Gross Breesen ... Bondy. Is he still alive?'

'No, I don't think so. He was quite a bit older than you.'

Harry nods.

'He was a good man.'

We don't stay out in the sun for much longer; the heat grows too much and the wind has picked up, so we decide to head back up to the room. Harry keeps closing his eyes and bowing his head, his hands resting softly clasped in his lap. I wheel him back through the cafe area, up the escalators and to the air-conditioned fourth floor. The room is just as we left it: the lights are off and it is cast in shadows; the TV is switched to a kids' cartoon channel. I notice that the lunch tray is gone and the bed is made.

'Would you like to sit on the chair, or get into bed?' I ask Harry.

'Bed.'

I help him into his bed, take off his velcro sandals and put a blanket over him. Below the TV on the small wooden cabinet are framed pictures of Max, Edith, Heinz and Irmgard, Lynn, and Harry's three children.

'Where is *meine Mutter?*' he asks me. I know that he knows the answer; it's hidden somewhere, but today he cannot find it.

'She died in the war a long time ago,' I say softly.

'Did you ever meet my parents?' he asks me.

'No, I didn't, I'm afraid.'

'You would have liked them,' he says. 'My father, he would talk to anyone. And my mother, too. They were good people.'

I nod.

'I should like to speak to them again,' he says.

His eyes soften and close, and he recedes into sleep. I glance at the framed pictures of Max and Edith, the centre of my months of fixation. To know them as he knew them would be an immeasurable gift, as precious a thought as it is impossible. I return to my laptop, looking over at Harry every few minutes, but he is fast asleep.

Between lockdowns, I make it to South Australia. I've never been and I figure it might be worth having a look around Kuitpo for traces of the old colony. The word colony itself makes me uneasy. The immigrants at Kuitpo were still part of the colonial project, clearing land for settler means. I don't know what I'll find—what I'm expecting might become clear by retracing these early steps—or if anything will be even faintly recognisable to the archived pictures I've found. Time shifts the meaning of place.

I step off the plane and into the terminal where a long line of officials sits behind foldout tables, each wearing a plastic shield over their face, checking every passenger's details. I shuffle forward in the line until I find myself face to face with one of these officials.

'Have you had any cold or flu symptoms in the last two weeks?'

'No.'

'Have you travelled internationally in the past two weeks?'

'No.'

'What is the purpose of your trip to South Australia?'

'University studies.'

'Okay, everything looks good. Have a nice trip.'

'Thanks.'

The official stamps my entry permit and motions to the exit, where another official stands, checking for the stamps. I make it out of the airport but cannot shake an uncomfortable feeling that travel will never return to how it was pre-pandemic. I am unnerved by the heightened surveillance and the mechanical structure of passenger vetting, even more intense than it was before.

Early the next morning, I walk into the centre of town, to the Adelaide Holocaust Museum, where I have an appointment with the curator Pauline Cockrill. She reached out to me because she found a piece I wrote last year about Kuitpo; she was researching this piece of history herself, and was thrilled that she had found someone else who was interested in it, let alone had a family connection to one of the refugee workers. Pauline asked if she could include Harry's story in the permanent exhibition at the museum, because the main audience of the museum is high school-aged students, and Harry was only a little older than that when he was at Kuitpo. For the exhibition, Pauline put together a 100-word summary of Harry's story, and asked me to send through a few pictures of him in his early years in Australia. Today, she is going to show me around, specifically the part of the exhibit that now features Harry.

The museum's facade is nondescript, except for a small plaque that identifies it as the Holocaust Museum. You cannot walk straight in from the outside; you must first buzz, and a security guard meets you at the door. The museum is in a part of the Catholic Church building that used to be office spaces. Pauline meets me at the door and asks if I would first like to go upstairs and have a chat. I follow her up the stairs to the second-floor office area. She has set up shop in a disused office space in the interim before it's restored. The offices look like they haven't been touched since the 1990s. The ceilings are low with panels of dim fluorescent lights. In each room are scatterings of mismatched furniture donated by the Catholic Church. It feels dark, almost forgotten. I am told that this second floor will soon be used as an education centre and gallery, and for curatorial storage. Pauline pulls up a seat for me and we sit alongside her desk, computer and a pale grey filing cabinet with a copy of Anne Frank's diary sitting on top of it.

We talk about Harry and his life leading up to his journey to Australia. We talk about how good it is that the museum features stories specific to South Australia. She tells me about another museum at Tanunda, the Barossa Museum. There's little mention there of the Nazi presence in South Australia, though certainly there were Nazis in the Barossa around the time Harry was living in the area. In the 1930s, the leader of this group was Dr Johannes Heinrich Becker, who emigrated to Australia in 1927, and joined the Nazi party in 1932. His following were mostly recent German immigrants, and Becker arranged for German propaganda films to be screened at Tanunda.

We wander through the exhibition of black-and-white pictures and artefacts of clothing donated by descendants, until we find Harry. Mounted on a display board is a picture of him at 18, wearing a white shirt and baggy, worn pants, standing on dusty ground littered with dead leaves.

The summary of Harry's story reads:

Eighteen-year-old Hermann Pollnow, only son of a specialist surgeon in Berlin, was one of six German-Jewish refugees who were selected to learn farming skills at Kuitpo. He was renamed Harry Peters by the Jewish Welfare Society office in Melbourne. After the war, Harry retrained as a doctor. Both his parents perished in the Holocaust.

I look at the picture for a long time. It looks different here in this museum, mounted next to pictures of other refugees, and relics. It feels strange to see Harry up on the wall, this part of his life as an exhibit. I feel a sense of pride, or contentment, or assuredness, that these few words of his story are preserved.

After the exhibition visit, I walk around the centre of the city, trying to picture it as it was when Harry was here, but it's difficult to look beyond what is in front of me. The lines of the footpaths and trees, the arched windows and stone buildings are perhaps a glimpse of what the city might have looked like. My picture is faint, darkened at its edges.

The following morning, Pauline and I make the trip to Kuitpo. Apparently, all that remains of the original building are two chimneys that were part of the men's recreation area. We talk intermittently while I scratch notes in my notebook. My words show traces of the dirt road, illegible and broken:

Blackened tree trunks, blue stretch of sky with clouds—could be a painting.

We drive through archways of stringy gumtrees, over crested hills and green fields. I try to imagine what Harry would have thought as he passed through this foreign terrain on his way to the colony. What must it have felt like to be so far from home?

As we drive, Pauline tells me that in her research, she discovered this area experienced horrendous fires in early 1939, akin to the Black Summer we experienced at the end of 2019.

'This land would have all been destroyed, and your grandfather would have been here for the aftermath,' she says.

She speaks of the more recent fires.

'The town I live in was badly affected, the flames came right up to the house and our two sheds, paddock fences and caravan were all razed to the ground. You can still see the black, charred line a metre away from our bedroom window.'

Pauline pauses, thinking.

'We were on our way to New South Wales the day the fires came. It was actually our neighbours who helped save our house, along with the water bombers and the fire service, of course.'

Pauline tells me that the wind miraculously changed direction, which averted the fires closing in on her town from two directions.

'I do feel immense guilt that we had a sketchy fire safety plan, and our house was saved, yet so many who were so prepared lost their houses.'

We continue in silence as I write notes intermittently.

'I think this is it,' says Pauline as she slows.

We've reached the red marker on Google Maps along Blackfellows Creek Road. The road is quiet except for a pair of magpies warbling on a telegraph pole. I hop out of the car. To me the place looks unexceptional, just another stretch of dirt road. Up ahead, an embankment of still water is skirted by overgrown grass, flickering in the wind. The sun is high, and I shed my jacket. I feel my skin prickle as a gust of wind shoots through the warmth. On my phone screen is the picture of Kuitpo Colony I found in the State Library of South Australia archive, which shows a few buildings positioned beside a lake, beneath a round hill.

From behind me, Pauline calls, 'Do you think this is it?'

'I'm not sure. It looks like it could be,' I reply.

I hold the picture up so it's side by side with my view. There is a resemblance in the landscape, in the undulations of the hills, the patches of grass and the dam, that pulls me in the direction of the past. I think this is it, this is the place, and I stand and squint and will myself to feel something. The prospect of this sort of archaeological discovery is thrilling, yes, to search and find, to be correct. Yet there's also an irreconcilable absence, the space between then and now, which impedes my vision of what was.

'If I'm not mistaken, I think the ruins should be a bit further down the road,' Pauline calls to me from back down near the car.

'At Kuitpo Colony,' taken approximately 1933, courtesy State Library of South Australia.

I finish taking my pictures and return to the car. Along the road are remnants of felled trees; their trunks jut out at staunch angles, and dead branches and blackened leaves litter the ground. It looks like they've been stampeded, pummelled to the earth by colossal force. I am struck by their hollowness.

'There they are!' I say from the passenger seat and point through the wound-down window to an unmistakable tower of cobblestones, one of two brick chimneys that were once in the colony's recreational room.

We walk quietly around the site, inching closer to the ruins. Leaves crunch underfoot. The soil around the chimneys is barren, hard-packed, dry. No sound but the wind. I try to conjure the walls, furniture, stoke the flames that warm the cheeks of men huddled together. No, not huddled, seated at wooden tables playing cards, writing letters, talking. Is that Harry I see, there, in the corner, reading over his letter from home? Does he, too, listen to the call of wind? Does it remind him, too, of the ocean?

We wander a little further up the hill until there's nothing left to see. I take one last look at the ruins. I wonder if they'll still be here in 100 years.

10

4 August 1939

Dear Mutzi,

Many thanks for your letter of 20 July, which arrived yesterday …

I want to say the following about your letter. I am very sorry that you are disappointed about your current employment. I have to tell you, though, I don't really understand your indignation. You wrote: 'We didn't imagine it correctly.' Well, you were wrong. Probably, the training farms look like that in Australia. If your one is supposedly the biggest and the best, you can imagine how the other farms might look. One probably should not apply European standards, as you know them from Breesen and Werkdorp, with their highly cultivated agriculture. It is a well-known wrong attitude for immigrants to apply their old standards to their new environment. One has to adapt. You want to learn something, bon. *I don't know anything about these things, but I can imagine, one can and should learn how to make the bush arable and harvest it. Once you settle, you will surely be provided uncultivated land… with tractors and so on. Also, I don't find the accommodation in wagons such a big deal; I had worse in 1914–1918, God knows, and I was a whole lot older than you. And you have been housed in worse and more uncomfortable places before as well, not so long but for more than three weeks.*

'Finally', you want to be independent and earn money? Funny, funny. It will take a little while, until you earn enough money to bring us over, quite apart from the fact that Mutti is still too weak to handle such a long trip. As for that daft comment that you'll only stay there for two months and then will find jobs on your own and eventually meet up with the others—although you know nothing about them yet—I'll show my disapproval by simply saying this: 'Nice, captain'.

But we are happy that you are feeling so well, aside from this, and that you're not planning on losing your sense of humour or your good mood. When you write next time, I would like to have a precise statement, detailing which of my letters you have received. In some, I've asked questions that need a response. Do you keep them for a while or do you throw them away instantly?

The new name is very funny; is that official or how does that work? Be honest! I showed the letter to Mutti and Oma, of course. There are no secrets. Most importantly, stay healthy—the main thing! What about the koalas? There was a funny joke in the newspaper recently, with a picture, from an Australian humorous paper. There was a kangaroo with an embarrassed or frightened look on its face, holding a paw in front of its mouth, and you could see a baby kangaroo somersaulting through the air. 'That's the third time this morning I've flown out. Can you please do something about your hiccups, Mutti?'

Thousand greetings and kisses in love,
Mutti and Vati.

*

Harry's decision to leave the Kuitpo Colony was carefully weighed up, culminating from weeks of deliberation and the conclusion that there was no prospect to further his skills nor earn more money than the five-shilling allowance. On the one hand, Kuitpo was a known place; in fact, it was the only place Harry actually knew well in the whole of Australia. He was with a group of fellow refugees who, while they never spoke of it, had similarly endured the psychological upheavals of the last few years. Individually, they carried their heavy memories around with them but did not dare bring them up or put them into words. It was an invisible camaraderie they shared, along with painfully recent memories of their old lives, their childhoods in Germany or Poland. On the other hand, Harry knew his friends and fellow Gross Breeseners in New South Wales, Jonny and Hanni Jonas in Berrima, and Eric at a farm on the Central Coast, were living in better conditions and with greater opportunity than he'd found so far at Kuitpo.

In a letter to the Welfare Society, Harry expressed his confusion at the accommodation in railway carriages and the discontentment among some of the refugees. When he was severely reprimanded for complaining, he decided it was time to try his luck somewhere else. Harry envisioned something better and was determined to find it, despite not knowing where he might next find himself. He had completed three months at Kuitpo and worked as hard as he ever had, even harder than at Gross Breesen, spurred by the need to prove himself worthy of Australia's charity.

On either side of the dirt road, gumtrees with thick trunks and branches stretched like an archway, their leaves rustling softly. A troupe of men walked down the road with axes slung over their shoulders, on their way to the timber forest. They nodded at the refugees, knowing them from Kuitpo but unwilling to strike up conversation. Harry felt the weight of his pack and the morning sun as he walked up the road, the uneven ground and relentless hills making his legs ache. He and the others made it to the stop just as the bus pulled up. Mud and dust were caked onto its sides and the windows were all wide open. The driver had a red face and, similar to his vehicle, dirt caked onto his button-up shirt. They piled into the bus, along with a smartly dressed woman and her son, and an elderly man in a white collared shirt and faded blue cap. They looked at the boys, with their dark hair and complexions and sheepish eyes, and immediately registered that they were not from around here. Locals knew from the papers that Kuitpo had taken in Jewish refugees, but they had not expected to be confronted by them in person.

'Good day,' Harry said to the bus driver, trying his hardest to mask his unmistakable German accent.

The outbreak of war was fresh, only weeks old. The Australian Government immediately categorised any refugee from an enemy country, regardless of whether or not they were Jewish, as an 'enemy alien'. Some were seized from the cities and put in prisoner-of-war internment camps, and some were unjustly vilified because of this hastily made government policy. Which is why the bus driver stared at Harry when he spoke, trying hard to recognise his accent, knowing only that it was different from his own. The driver then realised he was holding up the line of people waiting to board, so he nodded gruffly and kept quiet.

The bus ride to the city took about an hour. Mostly, they stared out the windows, relishing the hot wind on their faces and the sight of green hills that stretched as far as the distant horizon. They passed vineyards and gardens and pretty, solitary houses. So much land, so much space. The bus descended the Adelaide Hills until eventually they came to denser streets, with houses in rows and pedestrians traversing tram-lined roads. The buildings looked like the ones in London: banks and clothing shops and markets lined each intersection. The hills were always visible in the distance, even from the middle of the city, a reminder that here there was once only a vast plain connecting the foothills of those slopes.

'Thank you,' Harry said as he alighted the bus.

'Where are you from, boy?' the driver asked, as Harry stepped down onto the footpath and the other boys followed in his wake.

'Berlin,' he replied. The driver's eyes widened, his mouth half open. Before he could say anything, car horns bellowed behind him, and the driver hastily pulled away from the kerb. Harry watched the bus disappear into the traffic. There they were on the footpath, alone in the city. Having spent the past three months in the country where the only road was the dirt one used by scant locals and sporadic trucks leading to the colony, to be back in a bustling city once more felt foreign.

The boys dispersed, each with his own hopes of finding new employment. Harry wandered through Victoria Square in the direction of the marketplace. People were milling around the entrance, holding large parcels and paper bags full of goods, conversing in fast English. Farmers from all around came to the market to sell their produce and pick up what necessities they did not make themselves. It was Harry's intention to find one of these farmers and offer his labour in exchange for board and food.

With his pack still slung over his shoulder, he stepped into the market. The stalls snaked around in rows, each one full of people yelling their orders over the crowds. Heavy carcasses hung from metal hooks: whole birds and animal flanks, raw and stamped with red numbers. He saw fresh fruit and vegetables, pallets full of ripe apples and huge potatoes, confectionery, cakes and biscuits, hessian sacks full of flour, mountains of cheeses. The sour reek of bruised forgotten produce mixed with the odours of meat and fish and dust stung Harry's nostrils.

He bought a pack of cigarettes and wedged them into his front pocket. Above him on either side were signs fastened to thick wooden beams, painted onto timber planks with smart calligraphic letters for each stall. His eyes trailed a procession of large light bulbs hanging from wire down the length of each aisle, the electric spinal cord of this humming, breathing spectacle.

Harry walked as slowly as he could and strained his ears to listen to each person he passed. The conversations were often unintelligible, spoken in English so rapid and colloquial he had no hope of understanding anything. Others noticed him lingering and shuffled away, casting beady glares back at the strange young man who seemed purposeless among the chaos. Still, he kept wandering through the aisles. After his fifth lap around the market, Harry heard a booming voice that seemed to be speaking to him alone. He knew this was impossible, and yet the words flew to his ears with magnetic familiarity; so strong was this pull that his whole body spun around and shocked the couple walking behind him.

He scanned the direction the voice was coming from.

A group of men were gathered around a fruit and vegetable stall, clad in thick, grubby, button-up shirts, brown trousers and boots crusted with dirt. Harry walked towards them. His native tongue was unmistakable. It was a surreal experience to listen to it spoken so confidently in an Australian market. It was the first time since he had left home that he had heard German spoken by anyone but his fellow refugees, and even then, they were only ever game to speak it in hushed whispers. It was risky to speak the language of the enemy, especially when families of recently deployed soldiers were within earshot. He skirted the circle of men, who paused their conversation and turned to him.

'Can I help you?' said the man with the booming voice, in English.

In German, Harry replied, 'I heard you speaking German, sir, and I—'

'Couldn't help but eavesdrop?' the man said, then cracked

a smile. He glanced at Harry's pack, his hardened physique and brown complexion.

'When did you arrive?' the man asked, slipping into German.

'July, sir,' Harry replied. 'On the *Strathallan*.'

'Just in time. I hear the government's shut the doors now.'

Harry nodded. 'I've been working up at Kuitpo Colony.'

'Ah, yes, I know Kuitpo.'

'I have just left, actually. I completed my training there and am looking for work. Do you know anyone who needs a farmhand?'

'What kind of work can you do?' he asked.

'Anything, sir. I received full agricultural training back home. Mostly, I've been felling trees for the past three months.'

The man peered closer at Harry.

'How old are you?'

'Nineteen, sir.'

'Alright, then. I need a boundary rider on my property, someone to ride out, fix my fences, do some odd jobs, that sort of thing. Can you do that?'

'Definitely, sir!'

'Alright, good. Wait out the front and I'll come and get you. You can call me Mr Albrecht.'

'Mr Albrecht, my name is Her—Harry Peters.'

Thirty minutes later, Mr Albrecht emerged from the market carrying a tray of fresh vegetables and butcher's parcels. Harry, who was leaning against a lamp post with his eyes fixed on the entrance, waved and walked towards his new employer. Mr Albrecht motioned to a pale blue pickup truck a few metres down the road.

'Alright, put your bag in the back. The station's out at Norton Summit. I hope you don't mind speaking German; my wife's

Australian so I never get to speak it at home.'

'Sure, I don't mind,' said Harry, as he slammed the front passenger-side door shut. Albrecht started the engine and the truck slowly groaned into motion.

They sped along Norton Summit Road, east of Adelaide, the truck churning up dust in its wake. The edge of the road dropped off into steep bushland and trees, leaves limp in the dead breeze.

'We'll be making a brief stop,' said Albrecht.

The truck slowed as they reached a building, its front made of bricks and its back made of sandstone, with a timber balcony on stilts that wrapped around. Painted in block letters were 'Cool Drinks' and 'Afternoon Tea', and on a sign hung at the entrance was 'Scenic Hotel, since 1869'.

'Come on, let's have a drink,' said Albrecht.

Harry followed him into the pub.

Inside, the air was thick with cigarette smoke, and a billiards table stood in pride of place next to the front entrance. A few dazed-looking men leaned against the bar, their schooners perspiring on the wooden pass. They nodded to Albrecht and didn't seem to take a second glance at Harry. Albrecht went up to the bar and signalled for the barman, who set two pints of beer down in front of him. Albrecht took out a few coins from his pocket and put them on the bar. Then he motioned for Harry to follow him out to the deck. They sat at a table overlooking the hills. Albrecht took a long scull from his pint, smacked his lips and stared out at the countryside.

Harry took a modest sip.

'You can see my place from here, it's over there beyond that ridge.'

He pointed and Harry followed his finger.

'It's beautiful, isn't it,' said Albrecht, more to himself than to Harry.

'Yes, very beautiful,' Harry said.

'So, where in Germany are you from?' asked Albrecht, before taking a long gulp of beer. Harry mirrored Albrecht and took a gulp himself. He sat straight, squared his shoulders, observed the mannerisms of the man opposite him as one to emulate.

'Berlin.'

'What does your father do? Not farm work, I imagine.'

'He's a doctor. A surgeon, actually.'

'I see. And he couldn't emigrate?'

'No. He won't leave his work.'

Harry did not want to admit that his father could not afford to emigrate, nor that his mother was too ill to travel.

'And how did you manage to get out here by yourself?'

'I came with a group of students from home. They're at farms in New South Wales, and I was at Kuitpo with five other refugees. We all went to the agricultural school Gross Breesen in Silesia, and could get permits because of our skills.'

Harry was reluctant to go into further detail with Albrecht. He was still a stranger, after all.

'Well, you're helping me out of a real bind. I'm a man down, you see. And riding fences isn't the sort of job I can do myself. You'll be riding a pony day in, day out, sleeping out in a swag and you'll likely be away for weeks on end. But I'll treat you fairly, don't worry about that.'

Harry was in no position to protest, so he nodded and sipped his beer. Albrecht lit a cigarette and passed Harry the packet.

'This is a good country. If you work hard, you can go far,' said

Albrecht. 'You should feel very lucky to be here.'

'Yes, I do feel lucky,' Harry said.

As he looked out at the hills, cast in a softening blue haze, he knew he was lucky. But with this feeling of luck also came sadness for those he had left behind, those who had not been allotted his same good fortune. As Harry drew a cigarette, the two men sat together quietly, as a pair of invisible cockatoos argued in shrill squawks in a tree close by.

After a while, the sun began to set and Albrecht drained his third pint. He said it was time to get home and Harry followed him back to the truck. It was another 15 minutes to the sheep station, and the truck pulled into the property just as the sun slipped behind the hills. The station was built on a stretch of flat land with grass the colour of hay; it was home to hundreds of sheep that flocked together in the darkening evening. Harry was reminded of the land at Kuitpo—the same colours, blue, orange and pale green, which for him was the palette of Australia.

'Best that you wait out here, Harry. I'll go in and tell Mrs Albrecht about you first, so she doesn't get a shock.'

Albrecht went into his house, a small single-storey brick place with a tin roof and spacious front deck decorated with orange and purple blooms. Albrecht and his wife emerged soon after.

'This is Harry Peters. He'll be our boundary rider for the next few months.'

'Very pleased to meet you, Harry,' said Mrs Albrecht.

She was a short woman with wavy brown hair pinned in a neat bun at the nape of her neck. She wore a pale yellow apron with smudges of flour across the front. Harry guessed she was the same age as his mother.

‘Pleased to meet you,’ said Harry and bowed, a force of habit.

‘We don’t bow in Australia. Do I look like royalty to you?’ Mrs Albrecht smiled. She held out her hand and he shook it briefly.

‘Right. You’ll be on the porch.’ Albrecht motioned to a small mattress on the wooden boards near the front door. ‘It’s quite comfortable, and besides, you won’t be staying in it many nights.’

‘Our last man found it quite alright,’ added Mrs Albrecht.

‘Thank you. This will do just fine,’ said Harry.

‘Lamb’s fry for tea,’ said Mrs Albrecht, as she walked back through the front screen door.

The sun fell behind the hills, the stretches of fields and shrubs darkened and the sky beyond turned pink.

That night Harry, exhausted, fell asleep to the soft bleating of sheep, and the roar of cicadas and other insects he could not yet name. He hoped he had found a friend in Albrecht, or at least a reasonable employer, bound as they were by home country. He thought of the other boys who had left Kuitpo with him and hoped they, too, had found promising work. He lay still in the orchestral blackness and wondered what lay ahead.

Harry learned to tell the time by the sun’s position in the sky, the only way of documenting the passing of time when it was just him, his pony and the stretches of land and fences. He had been riding fences for nine straight days and sleeping in his swag, eating rations of bully beef and biscuits. He’d been under Albrecht’s employment for more than a month and had grown used to the solitary life of a boundary rider. Now he was on his way back to the station, having spent the better part of two weeks fixing fences and herding stray sheep. He was looking forward to a shower and a hot meal, and a long sleep under a roof.

He rode over a hill, following the fence until finally he could see the station and the homestead, dwarfed by the surrounding hills. It was late afternoon and his stomach growled. He felt a pang of grief as he thought of home; what were his parents doing at this moment? It had been months since their last contact. His thoughts were constant, especially now that he had no company but that of occasional strangers. No family or old friends.

Harry rode into the station. Albrecht was on horseback herding the sheep before nightfall. As Harry slowed to a trot, he watched Albrecht and some of his other men swerve on their horses to direct the flock. Albrecht spotted Harry and waved him over.

'A sight for sore eyes!' he yelled over the commotion of the sheep. 'How did you fare?'

'Yes, fine,' said Harry. 'More to repair but I made good headway.'

'Well, you'll be getting a mate soon. The man you replaced is getting out and I said I'd find him some work with me.'

'Getting out ... ?' Harry asked.

'Prison. He went away for a while. He's a bit of a larrikin, got himself into some trouble in town for this—' Albrecht shot his right arm up in a mock Sieg Heil. Harry's stomach sank. 'He's a bit of a Hitlerite, but I've known him since I first arrived, and he's got nowhere else to go. Reckon there's no place better for him than out riding fences.'

Harry was stunned. As far from home as he now was, and still he could not escape.

Harry had assumed Albrecht was well aware of the reasons for his emigration, but now his employer's position was suddenly unclear. Once again, Harry found himself at a loss as to what to do next. He thought he would be at Norton Summit for a while yet, but there was no way he was going to wait around for this new man, no matter how much Albrecht vouched for him. Harry decided that he would leave Norton Summit as soon as he had secured his wages, which by now, along with what he was able to save from Kuitpo, was enough for a train fare to New South Wales. He would go to Bunnygalore Farm near a place called Berrima, where his friends and Gross Breeseners Jonny and Hanni Jonas were, along with George Strong, who had been with him at Kuitpo, and with whom he'd kept in touch over these last months.

> *I was working on the farm Bunnygalore, which means 'many rabbits', in the Belanglo Forest. The man that owned the farm was Mr Newman, he was running a private bus service from Longueville to Wynyard, he was an ex-World War I lieutenant commander in the Royal Navy, and he was very good to us. Strict man, but very fair. There were three Gross Breeseners* [already] *working on his place. My good mate* [Jonny] *Jonas, Dr Jonas, who was a doctor also studied later, he was a full doctor and had to study five years again, and his wife Hanni, Gross Breesen girl,* [George Strong] *and I stayed there for about two years, I suppose. But we never discussed it. He* [Newman] *discussed it, because he was a keen World War I man, and he explained all the battles. He was aware of our history, and he was very tactful not to bring anything up. He was very good, as I say, good to us. But the atrocities, at that time, weren't known. The atrocities, by the time they came out, I was not there anymore. So these subjects weren't discussed much.*

*

Bunnygalore Farm, taken by Harry Peters, c.1941.

Bunnygalore was accessible by one dirt road carved out of the rock and shrub. From the Hume Highway, the 14-kilometre road down to the farm was nothing more than two tyre tracks in the dirt. Newman built parts of the road himself, cut out of rock leading down a steep hill into the gully. The road was only just wide enough for one car to go along, and the drop off the left-hand side plunged 100 metres to the ground. Jonny worked to clear more land, blew apart rock and trees with dynamite and pitched electric fences to keep away the rabbits. Bunnygalore was skirted by mountains covered in thick shrub and native trees, land not yet cleared. Some 800 metres above sea level, it was almost never unbearably hot, and the river never ran dry, not even in the depths of summer.

The war was well underway, and messages from home grew fewer. This fact was never far from their minds, though their surroundings could not be further from the world they had left behind. Each morning, from the deep crevice of the valley, they looked up to towering hills, haunting, shielded by the swathes of gumtrees that teemed with wildlife at every hour of the day.

Bunnygalore was noiseless, but never silent.

While the young men were fit and strong, ideal soldiers, they were not allowed to serve Australia overseas because by law they were enemy aliens, and aliens could not serve their new country. Even though they were stateless, because Germany had stripped them of their citizenship, in Australia they were not fully accepted, either. People were still wary of the refugees. Were they spies, sent by Hitler to infiltrate enemy territory? No Australian had more right to fight the Nazis than these boys, and yet they were stuck in safety, relegated to farm work, all the while told by their superiors how lucky they were to be away from the fighting, while their Australian counterparts took up the front line.

Newman escorted the refugees to the cinema at Bowral every week on their days off and paid them a small wage; alien labour came cheap. By now, working at the farm were Jonny and Hanni, Harry, George Strong from Kuitpo and Eric, who joined from another farm in New South Wales.

Harry and George's main task was to build a new road through the property. It would be named George's Pass, after George Newman, not after the George who would clear it with shovel and axe. After a modest breakfast of toast and tea, the two headed out to the site; the sky was a pearly pink, the sun was still soft behind the ridge. On a low-hanging gum a few metres away from the makeshift track, a black cockatoo sat observing the view from the cliff face. Harry slowed.

'Look, George.' He indicated the bird. Its black feathers pointed downwards, its wings hidden. It had a small tuft of yellow on its cheek and a short crest. Harry gazed at the bird for a few moments. It cackled and screeched, and its mate replied in identical tones seconds later, from across the valley.

Harry felt the heaviness of the wheelbarrow's thick wooden handles, which held two pickaxes, a shovel and a long-handled stoning hammer, the only tools they used to carve the road out of a wall of earth and rock. They continued on to where they had left off yesterday. It was a daunting sight, seeing the hard earth that would only be cleared by their sweat and aching muscles. But neither minded the hard labour; Harry enjoyed it, mostly. It allowed him to concentrate on the immediate task at hand: hands on pick, pick into earth. He relished the satisfaction of slow but definite progress. Out here in the bush he found a kind of peace from the unrelenting fear of what was happening in Germany. Each day without word from his parents heavied his heart. All he could do was try not to think of it, try not to imagine, fix his gaze on the ground in front of him.

Later that evening, the refugees sat together around the wooden table in their living quarters. It was after dinner, each held a lit cigarette, their work shirts loose. As they did most evenings, they were discussing the future. In the two years he'd lived in Australia, Harry had travelled from Victoria to South Australia, then to New South Wales, worked on three farms and become fluent in English. Bondy had instructed the Gross Breeseners to continue the agricultural mission of the collective, and they had done their very best. Yet after two years, it was becoming clear to the group, especially to Jonny, the eldest by ten years, that a lucrative future in agriculture would not be easily achieved. Prior to emigration, none of the refugees ever dreamed they would be agriculturalists or farmers; they had taken it up out of necessity, to escape the fates that so many now faced at that exact moment.

‘Of course, the training we had at Gross Breesen has got us this far,’ said Jonny. ‘But I think it is time for us to consider what we might like to pursue away from farm work.’

Jonny had already completed five years of medical training, so it was medicine he intended to pursue once the war was over.

‘Harry? What about you?’

‘Well, my father is a surgeon back in Berlin. I think I should like to follow in his footsteps.’

George and Eric, the youngest of the group, were quiet. Neither had given much thought as to what profession they might like to pursue once this phase of their lives was over. It was difficult to see past the war. But the conversations they had during these evenings planted in their minds the idea that perhaps there was more to life than what appeared immediately in front of them; that careers beyond farm work might be possible after all.

After the war broke out, all correspondence between Harry and his family had to be sent through the Red Cross Postal Service. Only 25 words were given to the sender, and each letter faced scrutiny from censors.

Deutsches Rotes Kreuz
Präsidium / Auslandsdienst 7. JUL. 1941*155568
Berlin SW 61, Blücherplatz 2

ANTRAG
an die *Agence Centrale des Prisonniers de Guerre, Genf*
— Internationales Komitee vom Roten Kreuz —
auf Nachrichtenvermittlung

REQUÊTE
de la Croix-Rouge Allemande, Présidence, Service Etranger
à l'Agence Centrale des Prisonniers de Guerre, Genève
— Comité International de la Croix-Rouge —
concernant la correspondance

1. Absender / *Expéditeur*: Dr. Max Israel Pollnow
Berlin N 4 Johannisstr. 8.
bittet, an
prie de bien vouloir faire parvenir à

2. Empfänger / *Destinataire*: Harry Peters
P. O. Box 37.
Bowral, New South Wales, Australia
folgendes zu übermitteln / *ce qui suit:*
(Höchstzahl 25 Worte!)
(25 mots au plus!)

Beglückt über Nachricht. Leider Mutti nicht besser und Oma der Nerven wegen im Sanatorium. Selbst gesund und viel beschäftigt. Schreibe bald wieder. Herzlichste Grüsse, Küsse.

COMITÉ INTERNATIONAL DE LA CROIX-ROUGE - GENÈVE
18 JUIL. 1941

(Datum / date) 29. Juni 1941.

(Unterschrift / Signature)

3. Empfänger antwortet umseitig
Destinataire répond au verso

Red Cross correspondence from Max Pollnow to Harry Peters, 7 July 1941.

Happy about news. Unfortunately Mutti isn't better and Oma is in the sanatorium because of her nerves. I'm healthy and busy. I'll write again soon. Fondest greetings, kisses.

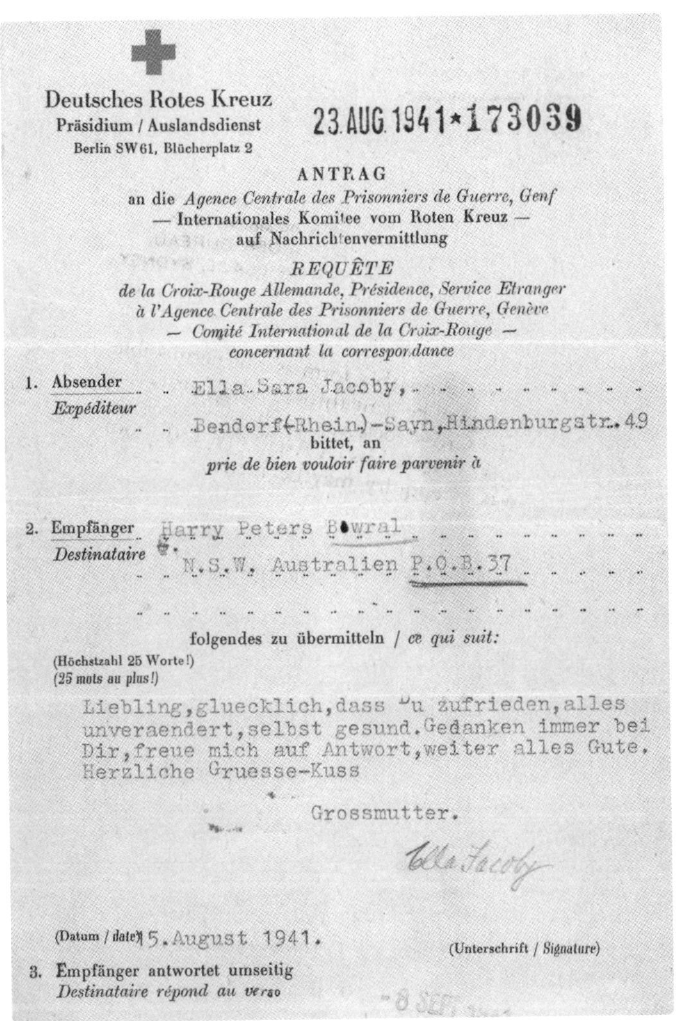

Deutsches Rotes Kreuz
Präsidium / Auslandsdienst
Berlin SW 61, Blücherplatz 2

23.AUG.1941*173039

ANTRAG
an die *Agence Centrale des Prisonniers de Guerre, Genf*
— Internationales Komitee vom Roten Kreuz —
auf Nachrichtenvermittlung

REQUÊTE
de la Croix-Rouge Allemande, Présidence, Service Etranger
à l'Agence Centrale des Prisonniers de Guerre, Genève
— Comité International de la Croix-Rouge —
concernant la correspondance

1. Absender / *Expéditeur*: Ella Sara Jacoby, Bendorf(Rhein.)-Sayn, Hindenburgstr. 49
bittet, an
prie de bien vouloir faire parvenir à

2. Empfänger / *Destinataire*: Harry Peters Bowral N.S.W. Australien P.O.B. 37

folgendes zu übermitteln / *ce qui suit:*
(Höchstzahl 25 Worte!)
(25 mots au plus!)

Liebling, gluecklich, dass Du zufrieden, alles unveraendert, selbst gesund. Gedanken immer bei Dir, freue mich auf Antwort, weiter alles Gute. Herzliche Gruesse-Kuss

Grossmutter.

Ella Jacoby

(Datum / date) 15. August 1941.

(Unterschrift / Signature)

3. Empfänger antwortet umseitig
Destinataire répond au verso

8 SEPT.

Red Cross correspondence from
Ella Jacoby to Harry Peters, 23 August 1941.

Darling, happy that you are content, nothing's changed, I'm healthy. Thoughts always with you, I'm looking forward to an answer, all the best. Fond greetings and a kiss, Grandmother. Ella Jacoby.

*

Excerpt from email exchange with the Jewish Museum in Berlin:

Dear Ms Scholfield-Peters,

Ella Jacoby nee Kempner (born 5 October 1874 in Görlitz) ... was a patient in the (Jewish) sanatorium in Bendorf-Sayn (close to Koblenz in West Germany). From December 1940 on, it was the only sanatorium all over Germany where Jewish patients were allowed to stay. The sanatorium was closed in 1942 and all patients deported to extermination camps in the East. Ella Jacoby was deported on 15 June 1942 from Koblenz to Sobibor and murdered there after her arrival. She didn't die a natural cause of death but perished in the Holocaust.

11

The Australian public did not see the full reality of the Nazi concentration camps until the first newsreels began to filter through internationally after liberation. And yet the worst excesses of the camps and Nazi brutality were reported in Australian newspapers from as early as 1933. Murders, pogroms, disappearances; the plight of Jews and other minorities in Europe was well known, and yet it seemed there was a dearth of empathy from the wider community for those few who made it to Australian shores. Certainly there were many advocates for refugees; while he was not well known at the time, one of the most significant was Indigenous activist Mr William Cooper, who, after hearing of the Kristallnacht pogrom in November 1938, organised a protest march to the German consulate in Melbourne to deliver a written condemnation of the persecution of Jews in Germany. This act of solidarity with the persecuted is considered to be the only one of its kind in the world to be carried out in the wake of Kristallnacht.

The popular sentiment towards Jewish immigrants in Australia, though, was one of hostility and suspicion. During the war, enemy aliens were fired from their employment, rumours spread of German spies posing as refugees, and many aliens, regardless of their religion, were subsequently interned in camps across rural Australia, where they were monitored and separated from the rest of society. Despite refugees very early on proclaiming their loyalty to Australia, and their gratitude for permission to settle in their new country, anti-refugee sentiment was still rampant in the Australian community, even within the established Jewish community. In reality, most refugees who fled Europe were anxious to show their appreciation for their new country, were hardworking and keen to make their allegiance to the Allies known.

In 1942, when the necessity for more manpower grew to an unignorable level, aliens were granted the opportunity to join the army via employment or labour corps. Harry signed up as soon as he could to serve Australia in the army. He was assigned to the Third Employment Company, one of 39 companies comprising 15,000 men. Eleven of the companies were made up of aliens, who were not permitted to bear arms or fight overseas. They undertook the labour necessary to keep the war machine going: maintaining barracks and machinery, delivering messages to other camps, manning store depots and handling cargo coming in and out of the wharves. The Third Employment Company was based in New South Wales; it was formed at Narellan in Sydney's south-west and later moved its barracks to Mascot, before eventually being absorbed into the airport. The labour corps brought immigrants from across Australia into one barracks, united by their otherness in the eyes of the government—despite many of the Italians and Greeks, themselves the children of immigrants, having been born on Australian soil.

Harry endured months of silence, receiving word from back home only a few times a year.

REPLY FORM Serial No. 81,294

AUSTRALIAN RED CROSS SOCIETY

MESSAGE SERVICE

(Through the intermediary of the International Red Cross Committee)

1. Sender—*Envoyeur—Absender.*

Name—*Nom* Dr. Pollnow

Christian Name—*Prénom—Vorname* Max

Street—*Rue—Strasse* Hindenburgdamm 11 bei Simon

Locality—*Localité—Ortschaft* Berlin-Lichterfelde

County—*Province—Provinz*

Country—*Pays—Land* Deutschland

2. Message—*Message à transmettre—Mitteilung.*

Hocherfreut über Nachricht vom Dezember. Wünchen viel Glück und Erfolg im neuen Beruf. Muttis Befinden ohne Besserung, selbst gesund. Denken Deiner stehts in innigster Liebe.

3. Addressee—*Destinataire—Empfänger.*

Name—*Nom* Peters

Christian Name—*Prénom—Vorname* Harry

Street—*Rue—Strasse* C/-Red Cross, 34 Martin Place

Locality—*Localité—Ortschaft* Sydney

County—*Province—Provinz* New South Wales

Country—*Pays—Land* Australia

4. Signature—*Unterschrift* Vati. Date, *Datum* 25.5.43.

Form to be detached and used for reply.
Detachez la forme et s'en servir pour la réponse.
Dieses Formular ist abzutrennen und für die Antwort zu benutzen.

22 JUIN 1943

Red Cross correspondence from Max Pollnow to Harry Peters, 25 May 1943.

Delighted with news from December. Good luck and success in your new job. Mutti's condition without improvement. I'm healthy. Thinking of you with the deepest love. Vati.

Max's telegram was sent on 25 May 1943. Nearly a month later, on 23 June, Harry's Aunt Irmgard Veit-Simon, who was not Jewish and was still living in Berlin, wrote to him. By this time, Irmgard's husband, Heinz, and son Rolf had been murdered; Harro, their eldest son, was in South America; Ulla, their eldest daughter, and Judith, the youngest, were in England; and Etta and Ruth, the only Veit-Simon children left in Berlin after 1938, were transported to Theresienstadt concentration camp soon after her telegram was written. Etta would survive, Ruth would not.

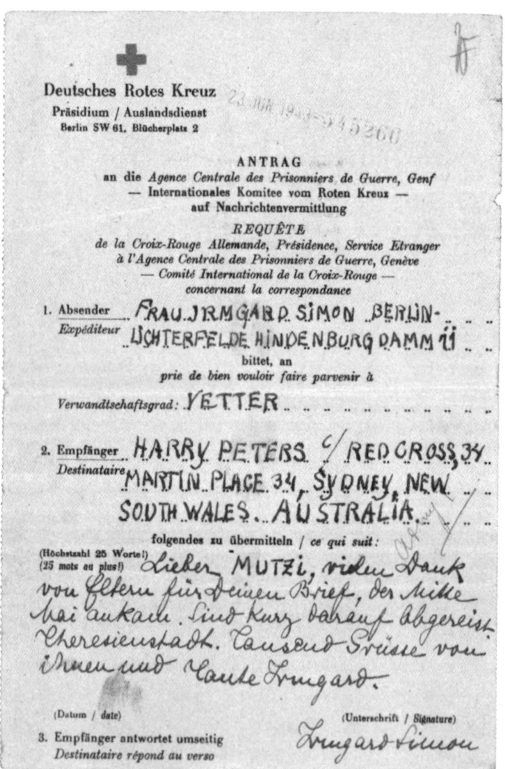

Deutsches Rotes Kreuz
Präsidium / Auslandsdienst
Berlin SW 61, Blücherplatz 2

ANTRAG
an die *Agence Centrale des Prisonniers de Guerre, Genf*
— Internationales Komitee vom Roten Kreuz —
auf Nachrichtenvermittlung

REQUÊTE
de la Croix-Rouge Allemande, Présidence, Service Etranger
à l'Agence Centrale des Prisonniers de Guerre, Genève
— Comité International de la Croix-Rouge —
concernant la correspondance

1. Absender / *Expéditeur*: FRAU JRMGARD SIMON BERLIN-LICHTERFELDE HINDENBURGDAMM 11

bittet, an
prie de bien vouloir faire parvenir à

Verwandtschaftsgrad: VETTER

2. Empfänger / *Destinataire*: HARRY PETERS C/ RED CROSS, 34 MARTIN PLACE 34, SYDNEY, NEW SOUTH WALES AUSTRALIA

folgendes zu übermitteln / *ce qui suit:*
(Höchstzahl 25 Worte!)
(25 mots au plus!)

Lieber MUTZI, vielen Dank von Eltern für Deinen Brief, der Mitte Mai ankam. Sind kurz darauf abgereist Theresienstadt. Tausend Grüsse von Ihnen und Tante Irmgard.

(Datum / date)

(Unterschrift / Signature)
Irmgard Simon

3. Empfänger antwortet umseitig
Destinataire répond au verso

Red Cross correspondence from Irmgard Simon to Harry Peters, 23 June 1943.

Dear Mutzi,

Thank you very much from your parents for your letter, which arrived mid-May. Shortly afterwards, they left for Theresienstadt. A thousand greetings from them and Aunty Irmgard.

Max and Edith were transported on 29 May 1943, four days after Max sent his last telegram to Harry. As a witness to the early brutalities of Buchenwald Camp, Harry could undoubtedly imagine what was in store for his parents, especially his mother, whose immune system was compromised by the slightest upheaval. Their cattle car transport left from Berlin Moabit station late at night, travelled through the night and arrived at Bohušovice station, Czechoslovakia, the following day.[39] The sick and incapacitated lay on mattresses on the ground of the cattle cars; Edith was one of them. This particular transport was mainly comprised of people over 60, who were either patients or nurses at the hospital in Auguststrasse, or the neighbouring old age home. Upon arrival at Bohušovice station, the transportees were forced by the SS guards to walk the two and a half hours to Theresienstadt Camp. Those who were unable to walk, including Edith, were driven. Edith's cause of death is unknown, but a safe assumption is that she died of disease and malnourishment on 28 July 1943, two months after her arrival at Theresienstadt. The last confirmed communication from Max was a coded telegram sent to Irmgard from inside the camp. It was kept and given to Hermann many years later, after the war.

*

I press play on the video testimony. I've reached the very end of the recording. The old footage wavers and the camera pauses on a small postcard, upon which is written a message in handwriting I do not recognise. I realise that all of Max's letters to Harry, up until now, have been typed. The interviewer speaks as the camera is fixed on the postcard.

'Tell me about this postcard we see here now,' the voice says.

Harry answers, his voice calm. 'This postcard is addressed to Mrs Irmgard Simon, from Berlin, and was sent from concentration camp Terezín[40] to her. It was sent from my father, Dr Max Pollnow, from Terezín.'

'Can you read it?'

'The postcard says, *Terezín 19 July 1944*. It was written by my father.'

Harry begins to read the card, and as I listen, my heart sinks.

'*Dear Irmgard, we hope this card finds you in good health. We always think of you, and we are well. We both of us work each according to his specialty.*' Harry pauses, and his tone shifts slightly as he offers an explanation to the interviewer.

'My father worked as a doctor in Terezín, and Mrs Simon's daughter, the other one, called Etta, was a graphic artist who used to do signs in the camp, Terezín.'

He continues reading the card.

'*Etta is specifically pretty and quite happy. Hopefully you have information from the aunts.*'

Another pause.

'That was a code that was agreed upon by my father and Mrs

Simon, when he knew that he was going to be transported from Terezín to Auschwitz. As far as I know, he was transported to Auschwitz on that day, 19 July 1944. It goes on to say ... *My boy* [Harry] *has his birthday on the ninth of August. I would have liked to write to him. We greet and kiss you a thousand times. Sincerely, Max.'*

Excerpt from correspondence with the Jewish Museum Berlin.

Dear Tess,

I'm afraid we do not have any materials pertaining to Max and Edith Pollnow in our holdings. I was, however, able to find in the collection of the Leo Baeck Institute in New York a drawing done by the artist Julie Wolfthorn in Theresienstadt of one 'Dr Pollnow', who I believe must be Max.[41]

On a sunny day in the first week of February 2021, Mum and I go to the nursing home to take Harry out. The home has a beautiful garden area and a path all around the property, so we can wheel him around as if we're beyond the gates. Today, he's in a good mood: he recognises us both, he's eaten well and he wants to go outside. He does not want to be in bed.

'Let's go then!' says Mum, grabbing his hat and sunglasses as usual. We trace the well-trodden route down in the lift, beyond the foyer and outside.

'Dr Pollnow', drawn by Julie Wolfthorn, June 1943, courtesy Leo Baeck Institute.

We wind around the path, which is lined with blooming flowers and thick shrubs. Harry reaches out to touch the flowers as I push him and Mum walks beside him.

'*Sehr schön!*' he says.

We follow the path around the line of self-contained retirement units, expensive ones that look onto the gardens, to a bench at the top of a grassy hill overlooking the whole complex.

'Up there, Tess, let's stop for a bit,' says Mum.

I wheel Harry up to the bench and together we lift him from his chair to sit down in the centre of it; Mum and I sit on either side. Mum clasps his forearm in her hands. We sit in silence for a while. Harry closes his eyes, not to sleep, but to enjoy the sunshine. It is peaceful in this spot, in this moment. I can tell he is calm and present. He is not distressed; he is just here with us, sitting.

'Oh, I like the sun,' he says.

Later, Mum leaves for a meeting and I stay with Harry until his evening carers arrive. He lies in bed, and I take out the photo albums for him to look at, but he is not interested. He looks exhausted, his mood has changed. I hold on to the memory of his face a few hours earlier, smiling and illuminated.

'Would you like anything to eat?' I ask.

'No, thanks,' he replies. 'I've got no pain,' he says after a long pause, a habitual response to the question asked by nurses and family constantly.

'That's good,' I say.

'I would like to see some friends that I haven't seen for a while …' he says.

'Which friends?' I ask, but he doesn't hear me. I sense he is somewhere else.

'You know, old friends.'

I am quiet, waiting for him to continue.

'I don't like to relax,' he says.

'Why not?' I ask.

'Well ... I just, don't like it. I'm used to getting dressed, going out, walking around town ... but I don't feel like it now. I just want to stay in bed, but that's not right.'

I sit and listen, trying to gauge his thoughts.

'Now I just look forward to closing my eyes and falling asleep. Which is not what I used to do, when I was young. I hope this phase will pass ... that I will get strong again. But I'm ...'

I watch as his eyes slowly fall shut again and his breath deepens.

During the days that follow, Harry is given palliative treatment and put on a steady stream of morphine, as a small gallstone obstruction is causing him unbearable pain. It is too immense for him to bear while conscious.

We are told that he will not wake up again.

He is still alive, but he is asleep, deep in medicated unconsciousness. A few days later, when I go to see him, I sense that it is for the last time. I enter the room and it feels different. Mum is there, sitting at the bay window, looking up at Harry every few seconds. His face is soft, peaceful, and a machine next to him makes a gurgling sound and beeps every few seconds. The room is dark; only dim natural light comes in through the windows. It feels as though all the emotion, all the pain of losing Harry, was felt in the last few months, and now there is just numbness. It is a strange feeling. He will not speak again; his 100 years of life, history and memories dwindle on the edge of presence. I do not cry as I have in the last few days leading up to this. I sit down next to Mum, who looks teary, but she doesn't break down.

After a few hours of sitting quietly in his presence, Mum suggests that I read Harry a bit of my work.

'But he won't be able to hear it,' I say.

'You don't know that.'

She leaves the room to give me some time alone with Harry.

I get out my laptop and sit on the armchair next to him. I don't quite know what to read, which part is the most significant, which part he would most want to hear. I know it's pointless; he is unconscious and without his hearing aids. But I feel a compulsion to read to him anyway.

'I know you can't hear me …' I begin. I look at him, at his resting expression. 'But I want to read you a scene I've been writing. You remember I've been writing about your life, about your parents. I know I've told you about it before … anyway, this is a scene I've imagined, I'm not sure if it actually happened like this, but I wrote it based on a letter your Oma wrote to you a long time ago. I've been reading all your old letters lately; they are really remarkable. The ones from your parents especially. I've come to really love Max and Edith.'

I glance at him again. I'm suddenly aware that this is the last time I will ever speak to him.

I begin to read.

*

Monday 9 August 1920
Berlin, Germany

Late afternoon light warmed the hospital room from the open window, yet the sounds of the traffic and people outside on the main thoroughfare seemed distant, quieter than usual. In fact, to Edith, at this moment, she and Max could have been completely alone. She registered nothing but the white pain in her belly and her husband hovering faintly above her. She could see him talking but his words flew over her head.

Her mother, Ella, was outside the room, waiting.

Edith closed her eyes and gave in to the agony that attacked her entire body. She wondered if this was how she was to die.

Edith drifted into unconsciousness, from the hospital bed to another place, a place where the sunshine bathed her face like warm water. She was lying on a beach of grey pebbles, salty water the same colour as the sky. She sat up and looked out to the horizon. She recognised the beach as Nice, in southern France, where she and Max used to holiday when they were first married. The beach was peppered with other tourists and children squawking at the water's edge, tossing themselves around, mirroring the waves.

To her left, Max was reading the newspaper. She looked at him with aching affection. She looked to her right and there was her mother, Ella, dozing in a wooden beach chair, fully clothed as she always was at the seaside, her large woven hat pulled down to cover her face. Edith felt an overwhelming sense of calm and safety. She reclined to lie back down and closed her eyes. She basked in the warmth of the sun.

How wonderful, she thought.

'Edith. Edith, darling, can you hear me? Pipchen?'

Edith's body was limp as Max frantically tried to wake her. Max touched her forehead, then pressed his stethoscope into her chest, relieved to hear a pulse. The nurse fetched a wet cloth and placed it over Edith's forehead.

'Edith, please, wake up. You have to push through this.'

Her eyes fluttered open suddenly and she saw Max in his white surgeon's coat, his brow furrowed, leaning over her. He squeezed her hand. The agony bore heavy on her body as she continued to push with all her remaining strength. With a sudden surge everything went white, and Edith was overcome with such aggressive pain that for a moment she could see and hear nothing. In that moment she felt only silence. Then, out of the whiteness, she heard the faintest sound, soft and small; somehow she recognised it immediately. Her heart swelled from it, and she willed it closer. It was a baby's cry, growing louder until she opened her eyes and gasped.

'It's a boy!'

Max cut the cord between Edith and the child, then handed him to the nurse, who wrapped him up in a blanket. Then she passed the tiny thing to Max, who looked upon him with gleeful adoration. He carefully placed the baby in Edith's arms.

Max went to the door of the room and beckoned Ella inside.

Ella went to her daughter's side and touched her forehead, looked upon the child. Max scooped him up and handed him to Ella. He looked on as Ella's face lit up; suddenly she was an Oma.

'What a perfect little boy,' said Ella, who could not have loved anything more than she did the little bundle in her arms.

She kissed his forehead and gave him back to Edith.

Edith looked down on her baby and felt something more powerful than she had ever felt. He cried but she did not feel distress; to her his crying was only more proof of the remarkable fact of his being alive. His face was speckled still with blood, and she used the swaddling blanket to wipe it from his tiny brow and cheeks. She saw Max in him immediately. Each feature was marked with a likeness to Max, from his wide, almond-shaped eyes to his nose and line of his mouth. But she was also delighted to see herself in the baby, a surreal recognition that would startle her in many moments to come. He was perfect.

'Hermann,' she said softly.

'Hermann Ludwig Pollnow, after his grandfathers,' said Max.

Dusk fell around them and baby Hermann drifted into sleep, his first sleep in this world, wrapped up in his bassinette at the foot of the bed. Edith, too, fell into her own exhaustion.

Later, Hermann stirred and began to gurgle. Max took the baby in his arms instinctively, holding him close to his chest. He would return to work tomorrow and their housekeeper, Frau Warnke, would become the baby's primary carer. He would work until very late each day and see the baby only when he was sound asleep, when he was already fed, had already been awake, even momentarily, to curiously study other faces, not his father's. He looked down at Hermann and marvelled at how small he was, and how much there was in this world for him to see, to experience. A baby softened even the most unsentimental man.

Hermann's eyes closed again, and he fell back asleep. Max softly put the baby in the bassinette, covered him with the blanket and kissed his forehead. He decided it was time that he, too, got some rest. He went to the basin, washed his face and hands, and changed into his bedclothes. He turned off all the lights in the small unit and made sure the doors and windows were locked. Then he went back to the bedroom where two bodies now slept, shut the door and turned off the light, so only Edith's dim orange lamplight illuminated the room. He left the lamp on in case the baby woke and he needed to rise swiftly. He manoeuvred himself into bed, rested his head on his pillow and let out a deep sigh.

Max, Edith and Hermann slept soundly together for the first time as Berlin hummed around them. Above their heads, the night was clear and warm, and the navy sky glittered with stars and streetlamps.

I look up from my laptop and see Harry resting. At last there is no pain. I gather my things, zip up my backpack and sit at the edge of the bed.

'Goodbye, Harry,' I say, and kiss his forehead. A shot of grief swells in my throat and I hold back tears. In moments so significant, every action feels inadequate. I hover next to him for a few more moments, committing to memory his peaceful expression. Then I pick up my backpack and leave the room.

Mum is waiting outside in the corridor. We embrace, then I take the lift back down and she returns to the room. I notice I'm shaking slightly as I cross the foyer and move through the glass doors out into the afternoon. I watch as other families make their way down the path from the adjacent carpark to see their elderly loved ones. I have an impulse to go back up, spend every minute

I can next to him, but I keep walking up the drive and out of the nursing home gate.

My memory of Harry is with me.

Max and Edith, too.

*

Do you think what you went through affected the way you lived your life?
Well, it has affected me in being aware of how precious life is, and to try and do the right thing. To take advantage of all opportunities and try and live a good family life. It hasn't affected me physically. But it has made me realise how lucky I was and how good my parents were to sacrifice themselves to let me go. To send me. And right through, I realise the good fortune that I've had since leaving Berlin. Or rather even in Berlin. That I've been shielded from the worst excesses that so many others had to endure.

Are there any messages you'd like to leave?
My children are aware of my past and are very keen for me to put it down on paper. They are very close to me and want to know all about my family and to strengthen the family ties.
One thing that these years have brought to the fore is that we are dispersed right through. I have family in America, England, not much here. But we are much closer. All this has brought the community closer together.
I always emphasise that to my children, to never to forget what has happened. It is important, I think, because the grandchildren, they are pretty young now, but in time they

should be made aware of their heritage. That's the message for the rest of the community. For the rest of the Jews, here and anywhere. Stay together. There is always a danger, when things are going well and one is accepted, as it was in Germany. I'm sorry to say that the Jews were not aware that they were Jews until Hitler came to power. I think that that should be prevented from happening again. That Jews should be made aware of their heritage. I think that's most important. On my part, I will try my best to leave my family's history in their hands, to pass on to further generations.

I stop in my tracks, take a few deep breaths of recovery and look back at how far I've come: up a steep incline of rocky steps that caused my legs and chest to burn. A year has passed since Harry died. It's mid-summer again yet the icy air persists; sharp and thin, it prickles my cheeks and nose and rips at my windbreaker. I'm captivated by the wildflowers in full bloom, cascading in vibrant bursts of purple, pink, yellow and white, down the green-brown facade of the mountains. I've never visited Kosciuszko in the summertime.

At the mountain peaks, jagged rocks jut out at every angle and massive boulders collapse into each other. I watch the flowers shiver. Leopard-print butterflies hover above the heath and march flies dart in frenzied bursts, carried by the wind. I breathe in the scent of the wildflowers and the mountain air, the exhilaration of high altitude, and the wondrous silence. I feel as though I am suddenly privy to another world, an observer of secret beauty and nature's interconnectedness.

The Snowy Mountains of Kosciuszko was Harry's favourite place. He was a keen cross-country skier and worked as a resident doctor at Charlotte Pass ski resort for many seasons. Harry first went to the snow in Australia after the war, in the 1950s. He was already an expert skier; he learned young and his love of it endured. Harry took his children to the snow most seasons, a tradition that was passed on to his grandchildren. Most family anecdotes have some relation to the snow. Harry's love for this place is now mine; I like to think I share his love of the cold blue sky and the roaring quiet.

The Kosciuszko Trail, taken by the author, February 2022.

Kosciuszko was as close as he could get to the mountains, forests and alpine landscapes he grew up with. Perhaps in the muscle memory of skiing there retained some expression of his old self, his old life. There's an element of escape here too, away from the city. Painful thoughts are whisked away by the fast breeze and dwarfed by the silent, magnificent mountains. I think of Harry and I think of the snow, his competitive streak, his absurd fitness level to be able to cross-country ski well into his 80s.

Harry is defined by this place, by adventure and family and natural landscape and physical endurance. He fought with Herculean strength to be this man, far from what was done to him in his early life. He began life in Australia as a stateless refugee who lost his parents to genocide. He was forced to renounce his old life and, over many years, build himself a new one. For Harry, the only way to do this was to work as hard as he could, to literally never stop. Mum and I both recall Harry telling us individually that to be successful in life you had to find what you are good at and be the best you can be at it. Eric, Harry's best friend, wrote in his memoir that Harry had a work ethic that rivalled the Clydesdale horse, Boxer, in Orwell's *Animal Farm*. It is unsurprising, then, that Harry worked through the war years in various jobs for the Third Employment Company, as a sapper and a diesel engineer. After four years of service, he had to leave the army in 1946 because of the deterioration of his right ear. Harry struggled with partial deafness even in childhood and by early adulthood he had developed a tumour on the right side of his head. Harry was bed-bound in Concord Hospital for two years, which, for a man so driven by action, would have been physically and psychologically devastating. But by this time, Harry had decided that he was going to pursue medicine, so he studied the required material for the entrance exam and sat the exam from his hospital bed—and was accepted into medicine at the University of Sydney.

In 1947, as he was beginning his degree, Harry met Helen Bridgefoot, a beautiful young journalist for the *Sun* newspaper. They were married after just three months. As Mum tells it, Helen saw in Harry a brilliant but troubled man who desperately needed a new start in life. She gave him this new life; she supported Harry through his medical degree, and together they had three children: Lindsay, Cathy and Julia.

Their marriage ultimately did not survive, though they spent over 20 years together. There were many reasons, but the early years were marked by Harry's undiagnosed PTSD and Helen's disappointment with a life she thought she wanted. I never really knew Helen, my grandmother, but I have always felt a strong affinity with her. To me Helen was a strong, intelligent, creative, brave woman who was trapped by the circumstance of her time. She put her career as a journalist to one side to have a family. In pictures of Helen, I see features inherited by Mum and her siblings: cheekbones, hairline, lips. I see them in myself, too.

Helen and Harry lived in Sydney first, then moved to Corrimal, a small town on the New South Wales South Coast, where Harry had been offered a job as principal of a general practice. While there was a big Italian migrant population, Corrimal was about as far as you could get from metropolitan Europe. For Helen, who was used to the fast-paced life of a Sydney journalist, Corrimal was the end of the earth. When it came time for their eldest, Lindsay, to attend university, they moved back to Sydney, and Harry was appointed medical superintendent and medical administrator of the Prince of Wales and Prince Henry hospitals.

That same year, 1973, Harry met Lynn. As Lynn tells it,

there was an electricity between them, a feeling she has never forgotten. They fell in love almost instantly and were inseparable for the rest of Harry's life.

Harry was awarded a Medal of the Order of Australia (OAM) for services to medicine in 1986, specifically for his role as medical administrator for the Prince of Wales Hospital. He continued his medical career for decades; in his later years, he transferred to medical legal work until he retired at 92.

It's difficult to distil a 100-year life into so few key moments, when every life is the sum of so many. I continue along the trail as I head for Charlotte Pass. I pass Seamans Hut, the solitary emergency outpost and site of many family anecdotes about getting stuck in a blizzard at the top of the mountain. I walk on, descending the hill and through the plains, passing over the Snowy River. Between the foothills of the main range, the midmorning sun cuts through the wind and I think of how much Harry would have loved this day: the sun on his face, the alpine air, the feeling of being home.

Mutzi and the author, c.1996.

Epilogue

Memories, of course, are contested ... Nowhere is this more clear than in the center of Berlin, where every site is a battleground of clashing nostalgias and future aspirations.

—Svetlana Boym[42]

We arrive in Berlin—Mum, Aunty Cathy and I—on a gloomy evening in early October 2022. Rain threatens overhead as we climb into a taxi at the airport; as we hurtle down the highway towards the city, the clouds open and a downpour throttles the windscreen. I receive a message from a friend in Berlin saying welcome, and thanks for bringing this lovely weather. Our driver asks us where we come from.

'Australia,' Mum replies.

'Australia! Very far,' says the driver. 'About as far as you can get from Berlin.'

In my experience this is the invariable response from Europeans upon hearing where I come from. Mum asks the driver if he's ever visited Australia and he chuckles, shaking his head. Too far away, he says. Eventually the highway disperses into a maze of streets and unintelligible signs. We slow into dense traffic. We're staying in a flat in Schöneberg, a large neighbourhood that stretches from Tempelhof to the Tiergarten. As we plunge further into the city, I'm struck by the abrasive concrete blocks of Soviet-era flats and the grey of the footpath, buildings, and sky, heavy with impending winter. We turn right onto Grunewaldstrasse, our street for the next week, and it's surprisingly wide, with tall, ornate apartment buildings and lines of trees on both sides. We slow out the front of a sage-coloured building speckled with tags and weather-worn posters.

'This is it,' says Cathy.

'Enjoy your stay in Berlin!' says our driver. I hop out on the footpath side and stretch my arms for the first time in hours. To my right is a table of people out the front of a closed cafe, smoking and drinking pints. To my left is a row of closed shops shadowed by the glow of the warm apartments above. It's quiet, I think, and then remember it's Sunday.

Our apartment is classically beautiful: high ceilings, hardwood floors, narrow kitchen with a window that looks down on an interior courtyard. Bathroom with a washing machine and dryer sandwiched in the corner, another randomly placed bathroom between the kitchen and living room and, my favourite feature, two large living room windows that open onto the street. I open one and lean out of it, feeling the cold night on my cheeks and neck. The rain has stopped but its trace remains on the leaves of the trees across the street and the black patent asphalt. I long to feel at home in this city, to speak its language, which is not so much German as it is U-Bahn lines, artistic expression, the pulse of a million cultures and living, breathing history. It's also the city that swallowed Max and Edith and exiled Harry, stamped out their centuries-old German lineage. I can feel Harry watching me as I look out over his old home with longing. I hear his words: 'Why would you want to live there? It's just a big city, full of ghosts.'

After a quick meal of kebab and lentil soup at a Turkish restaurant around the corner, I fall into an easy, deep sleep, and the street below is still.

If you walk around Berlin for any stretch of time, you will come across small brass squares in the footpath engraved with a name, date of birth, date of deportation and date and place of death. They are Stolpersteine (stumbling stones): a large-scale art memorial project by German artist Gunter Demnig that now spans Europe. The stones are laid at the request of descendants and other groups, on the footpath outside the last place of residence of Nazism victims. In 2023, the project celebrated the laying of its 100,000th stone, a staggering figure considering each stone is engraved by hand and the operation is entirely volunteer-run.

I learn from my research that in recent years there have been instances of defacement, and some stones have even been ripped from the street. Four years ago, we applied to have stones for Max and Edith laid outside Johannisstrasse 8, the flat they lived in from 1938 till their deportation to Theresienstadt in May 1943. Early this year, we received a response: our application was successful and the stones would be laid by Gunter Demnig himself on a day in early October. We had the option to have a cantor sing the Kaddish, the Jewish prayer for the dead, and an instrumentalist to accompany Gunter as he dug up the cobblestones to make room for Max and Edith's plaques. We aren't Jewish and Max and Edith were non-practising, yet it feels right to have the Kaddish sung.

'Okay, so we'll visit Johannisstrasse first and then the Pergamonmuseum,' says Mum over coffee and a bagel at the Italian cafe below our flat. Shana, a volunteer for Stolpersteine and an academic here in Berlin, has assisted us in organising the ceremony, and has stuck flyers on all the buildings along Johannisstrasse. The flyers are in German and outline Max and Edith's story alongside each of their pictures, and extend an open invitation to attend the ceremony. We decide to visit the street today to work out where we'll put the cellist and cantor. I'm eager to get a feel for the place, see their old front door and the surrounding buildings; to stand where they stood.

We turn onto Johannisstrasse, a relatively narrow street with a line of parked cars crammed down the right side. There is construction happening about 50 metres down the street and groaning trucks are passing through every minute or so. On each side, the buildings are shades of speckled concrete, some painted white, some beige, and the footpath is striped with two outer rows of cobblestones, interspersed with small green patches of defiant weeds. It looks to me like a typical inner Berlin street, yet as I walk along the footpath I feel a kind of reverence, as though I'm close to a grave site.

'No,' I hear Mum say from a few metres ahead of me. I walk over to Mum and Cathy. They stand on the threshold of number 8, beneath the arched entrance way, in front of the green double door. On either side of the entrance, where two ceremony flyers were stuck, only the double-sided stickies and the torn paper edges remain.

'Someone's ripped them down,' says Cathy.

Mum touches one of the remnant bits of paper. 'Who would do this?'

I look down the street and notice there are no flyers. Shana told us she had papered the whole street.

'Maybe drunk kids ripped them down,' I suggest, but I am unconvinced. None of us expected there might be opposition to Stolpersteine. I trace the bit of ripped flyer with my forefinger and sense the force with which it was torn. Violence hangs in the air around us and suddenly I feel unwelcome here, watched by the tall grids of square windows all around me. I look up and down the street in search of an explanation.

'Let's just go,' says Mum. We turn off Johannisstrasse and I feel uneasy, right to my core.

From where we are it's about a 20-minute walk to the Pergamonmuseum, one of the five museums on the Museumsinsel (Museum Island). All I know about the Pergamon is that it's home to the Ishtar Gate of Babylon, built by Babylonian King Nebuchadnezzar. Babylon fell in the sixth century BC and the city slowly crumbled, its remnants found centuries later by German archaeologists in modern-day Iraq.

The museum is packed with tourists, as we knew it would be. We collect our prebooked tickets and join the queue for our time slot. I flick through the museum brochure and trace the floor map. The museum is split into two levels: the first is Architecture of Antiquity and the Ancient Near East, including archaeological finds from the Roman Empire, Syria and Turkey, Uruk and Habuba Kabira, Ancient Iran, Assyria and, highlighted in red, Babylon. The second level is dedicated to Islamic cultures: Syria, Jordan, Egypt, central and south Asia, the Alhambra Dome with accompanying graphic. I'm overwhelmed by the immense breadth of time and place mapped by this one page of explanatory floor plan. This collection of ancient artefacts is one of the most significant in the world and yet is a drop in the ocean compared to the worlds that lie dormant beneath us still, undiscovered.

We follow the procession of tourists through the exhibition rooms, which are distinctly darker than the museum foyer and with little fresh air. I'm trying to focus on the exhibits and the voice of my audio guide, but my mind is distracted by this morning. I'm finding it hard to drag my thoughts away from the torn-down flyers and the heavy feeling that our family is not welcome here. Then I turn a corner and all of a sudden I am dwarfed by the Processional Way of Babylon. It is impossible to think of anything but the sheer magnitude of the walls, which, according to my guide, were three times as wide in Babylonian times. The walls are a tapestry of the real ancient bricks and modern replicas that fill in the gaps. I walk through the Processional Way, my neck craned, which leads me to the magnificent Ishtar Gate. The richness of the blues, greens and golds, the intricate floral ornamentations that skirt its edges and, I think, the incredible age of the thing, almost buckles my knees. I take a seat on the bench in the centre of the room and look up at the gate, sit still in its presence. How can this all have been resurrected from the ground? I wonder, my neck still craned. What must it have been like to find the first brick, then the second, then realise that you're standing on an entire civilisation? Sometimes I remember that every being that has ever lived on earth is still here in some form, packed underground, miles below cities, in oceans, in dust, in the wind.

In another exhibition room I find a plaque next to an aerial black-and-white picture of the museum, which, I read, was taken immediately after World War II. The buildings of Museum Island were largely destroyed by artillery fire and air strikes. Miraculously, the Pergamonmuseum survived without significant structural damage, though the glass dome ceiling shattered and the exterior walls were blackened by bombings and rubble. Parts of the roof were firebombed, exposing much of the collections – including the Ishtar Gate – to the elements. I feel something like grief looking at the burnt-out Pergamon, even though it was restored after the war. I feel grief for the thousands of museums, libraries and cultural archives around the world, razed to the ground without a second thought. The profundity of loss is too great to begin to conceive.

I find Mum and we both agree we've had enough. We sit on the long bench in the museum foyer and wait for Cathy.

'How are you feeling?' I ask Mum.

'Okay. I don't know, I still feel quite sick about this morning,' she says.

'Me too.'

'I know it was probably kids, but I just feel a tension here.'

I nod.

'I could never live in Berlin,' Mum says, and in that moment I feel naive for thinking I could. 'It must be hard for the youth here, carrying it around.'

On the way home from the museum it starts to rain again. We decide none of us can face the public transport commute home, so we call an Uber. A red Toyota Corolla pulls up and we clamber in; Cathy sits in front.

'English?' she asks.

'Little bit,' says our driver.

Cathy persists. 'We've just come from the Pergamonmuseum. Have you visited?'

'No, but I think they have a lot of things from Iraq. Ancient civilisations.'

'Yes, they do,' says Cathy.

The driver nods. The automated voice directs in German. We turn left, following the traffic, red and yellow lights bleeding into the window. Cathy asks the driver if he's lived in Berlin for a long time as the roads must be difficult to learn.

'Seven years,' he says. 'I'm Kurdish, from Iraq.'

Cathy nods.

'I work also as a bus driver here,' he adds.

'Oh, great,' says Cathy.

The driver tells us that it took five years to get residency because they—Germany—couldn't understand why he didn't want to go back to Iraq. They told him it was safe.

'I was living in Baghdad for 45 years. After 2003 when the USA occupied Iraq, they destroyed our society. Now we have maybe 20 militias in Iraq. If you go against the militias, they tell you to leave or they'll kill you. They told me 24 hours, if you don't leave your house, we will kill you. My neighbour refused and they killed him.'

'That's awful. I'm sorry,' says Cathy.

We each hang suspended in the quiet.

'Do you like living in Berlin?' asks Mum, after a minute or so.

The driver pauses. 'Berlin is a good city for refugees. There are a lot of different cultures here. But I know some people who have been waiting 20 years for residency.'

'It's no better in Australia,' says Mum.

'How long did it take you to learn German?' asks Cathy.

'Five years, but I am still learning.' He pauses. 'I think it was Oscar Wilde who said, life is too short to learn German.'

We all laugh. 'That's very true,' says Mum.

When we arrive back at the apartment, I am exhausted. I've been burning through nervous energy all day, worrying that something will happen to ruin the ceremony. We've printed off 15 copies of the flyer in case neighbours or passers-by want one, though I'm now unconvinced that anyone is going to turn up. We are all cheerful over dinner but I think that, individually, we are each apprehensive about what tomorrow will bring.

We stand once more in front of Johannisstrasse 8: Mum, Cathy, my cousin Vic who flew in last night from Zurich, and myself. It's 10am, an hour before the ceremony is scheduled to begin. A woman walks towards us, waving.

'Shana?' asks Cathy.

'Yes, hello!' the woman, Shana, replies. We shake hands with Shana, introduce ourselves and thank her for all her efforts, especially with papering the street. Mum tells her about finding the flyers torn down and Shana tells us that unfortunately it's a common occurrence. It depends on the neighbourhood, she says; it's always hard to predict what the response is going to be. We walk to a coffee shop nearby, around the corner and up the street, towards the synagogue. As we walk, Shana points out the one flyer that remains stuck to a building entrance. The text is bleeding slightly from last night's rain and the black-and-white picture of Max and Edith has turned patchy blue. Still, it's a small comfort to know that this one has stayed up despite the elements.

At 10.50 we stand out the front of number 8, waiting for Gunter. Shana tells us we'll recognise him when we see him, he's hard to miss. He'll be wearing a felt brimmed hat and a bandana around his neck. A van pulls slowly up to the kerb and a tall, burly man with hair to his shoulders steps out first. He's carrying four buckets: one filled with tools and the others filled with grey powder; I guess it's what is needed to patch up the footpath after the stones are laid. This man walks up to us, nods, smiles and sets down the buckets. There's a variety of picks, a mallet and spade, a leveller, all grubby and well used. In an instant the footpath is transformed into an artist's workspace. The man returns to the van, speaking into the back compartment, then another man hops out. He's smaller than the first, with grey straw-like hair and a beard, wearing an old denim shirt and brown suede vest, a brown felt hat and a red bandana around his neck. I also notice a large, cushioned kneepad strapped to his right knee. Shana was right; this man is unmistakably the artist, Gunter Demnig.

He comes and stands next to us, and we each shake his hand and introduce ourselves. He nods and says hello quietly, then turns to begin his work on the footpath.

'Should we start the cello?' Mum asks. It's slightly awkward to conduct your own ceremony on a public footpath. Gunter says yes, you can start, so Cathy gives a thumbs up to the cellist and she begins to play as Gunter kneels on his padded knee and begins chipping away at the cobblestones. I feel slightly put out by how quiet Gunter is; he has barely uttered a word to us, and his attention is turned completely to the project of digging up the footpath. Then I remind myself that he's been doing this same thing for two decades and, as Shana informed us, he's laying 12 different Stolpersteine today alone. There is simply not enough time.

The cellist begins to play a mournful, beautiful Bach piece and the thud of Gunter's pick and mallet echoes down the street. A few passers-by stop to watch. Gunter removes a patch of ten cobblestones right at the doorstep of number 8. I'm surprised by how shallow the footpath is, how near we are to the dirt. Max and Edith's Stolpersteine are two brass squares, ten by ten centimetres. Compared to the older blackened ones I've seen around Berlin, these are gleaming like polished jewels. The cellist stops playing and we listen in silence to Gunter as he lays the Stolpersteine, fills the surrounding gaps with the old cobblestones and softly thumps everything back into place. He whispers something to the stones; I can't pick up what it is. Then he slowly stands up, nods to us again, turns and walks back to his van. The whole process takes about 15 minutes. I look around at the watching group: us and Shana, the cantor from the synagogue and a handful of other people who were walking past and decided to stop. Shana says a few words about the project, then Cathy says a few words about our family, about Harry, and about how he would tell stories of Max and Edith to herself, Mum and Lindsay when they were kids. Cathy tears up at the end of her speech. I look at Mum, whose face is marred with grief, and realise this is Max and Edith's funeral. Cathy finishes and I take her place next to the stones.

> *Thank you to everyone here today, to Gunter Demnig for his years of service with the Stolpersteine project, and to Shana for organising everything. Max and Edith Pollnow lived here from 1938 until their transportation to Theresienstadt in May 1943. At this time, Max was working as a doctor at the Jewish hospital on Elsässer Strasse and Edith was bedridden and very sick with multiple sclerosis and pernicious anaemia. Edith's mother, Ella, visited this flat frequently and they had live-in maids, Fräulein Selma, and later, Frau Hanna, who assisted with Edith's care as well as housekeeping.*
>
> *Harry, who was then Hermann, stayed here for two nights after his imprisonment in Buchenwald and before his train to Holland, where he waited for a permit to eventually emigrate to Australia. This flat is the last place Harry saw his parents when he left Germany in 1939, though Max and Edith kept living here for four years after that time. During those years they wrote to their son every week, sometimes more. This letter collection has been preserved, so thankfully we know a lot about Max and Edith's life during these years.*
>
> *Our family is here today because Max and Edith gave their lives so their son could make it to Australia. It's a significant moment for us to be back here now, and to have their names permanently enshrined on the footpath in front of their last house.*

Stolpersteine for Max and Edith Pollnow,
8 Johannisstrasse, Berlin.

Walking away from the stones feels strange, like we're leaving Max and Edith behind. There isn't really closure here, no neat resolution. A plaque in the pavement doesn't change what happened, and remembrance of genocide has not hindered humanity's capacity nor proclivity for it. Max and Edith are two people out of many millions lost, whose names have been salvaged from the wreckage; yet these threads of memory are tenuous, even when cemented into the ground. I wish that Harry were alive to see them here, but then perhaps for him the grief would be too acute. To be back here at the place where he said goodbye to Max and Edith and everything, to have truly known them, the profound chasm between that time and now might have been too painful to bridge. For me the grief of this moment is nebulous; it is not specific, as it would be if these stones represented the murders of my own parents. It is a grief that extends beyond my family, across borders and time, borne from a heavy conscience for all those lives extinguished for nothing, all those names beneath the rubble.

We keep walking. I glance back down Johannisstrasse and see a couple of young women outside number 8, looking down at the footpath. Perhaps they live in the building, or perhaps they're staying at the hostel across the road. They look at the plaques for a few moments, then up at the front door. I could be imagining it, but the moment feels solemn. They look down once more, then turn and walk in the opposite direction, disappearing around the corner.

Characters and omissions

One of the main challenges of this project was choosing which individuals and events to include in the text. It is nearly impossible to cover every detail of a lifetime in one book, so choices about what to include and omit were crucial to the development of this work.

Harry's closest childhood friend was Alfred Gotthelf. He lived only a few streets away when the Pollnows lived at Altonaer Strasse. They kept in touch all through the 1930s, while Harry was at Gross Breesen and while he was awaiting his Australian emigration permit in Holland. During this time, Alfred was with his parents in Paris. Harry and Alfred planned to meet in Paris in April 1939; Harry even received a leave of absence from Nieuwesluis. However, this reunion never happened, presumably because it was too difficult for Harry to obtain a French visa at that time. Alfred emigrated to America and they lost contact, which Harry regretted deeply into old age.

Harry's closest friends at Gross Breesen and into later life were Erich Bacharach (later Eric Baker), Jonny and Hanni Jonas and George Strong. They all travelled together to Australia on the *Strathallan* and *Slamat* ships. On board the *Slamat* were 15 Gross Breeseners: Pitt, Herko, Erich, Leo, Klaus, Werner, Spitz, Waschi, Franz, Erwin, Fritz, Hans, Herbert, Hanni and Inge. On the *Strathallan* with Harry were Jonny, Rudi, Bosi, Günther and Kurt. While these characters are peripheral in this text, they were close friends of Harry's, and were his surrogate family in Australia.

The focus of this work is Max and Edith and their correspondence with Harry. Their letters underpin the central narrative; however, there are many more letters from Harry's friends mentioned above. I wish to acknowledge them as important people in Harry's early life. I hope I have been true to the voices and experiences of those included in the text.

References

1. Wolf Simon Matsdorf was a former Gross Breesener and Jewish migrant. Wolf Simon Matsdorf, *No Time to Grow: The Story of the Gross-Breeseners in Australia*, Sydney: University of Sydney, Mandelbaum Trust, 1994.
2. A. Hirschberg in *C.V. Zeitung* (Berlin-based Jewish newspaper, official organ of the C.V.), 1933, referenced in J. Boas, 'Germany or Diaspora? German Jewry's Shifting Perceptions in the Nazi Era (1933–1938)', *The Leo Baeck Institute Year Book*, vol. 27, no. 1, 1982, pp. 109–126.
3. The Survivors of the Shoah Project was a series of over 56,000 video testimonial interviews conducted by the University of Southern California (USC) Shoah Foundation. The project was founded in 1994 by Steven Spielberg as a means of preserving the testimonies and stories of Shoah witnesses and survivors.
4. While Harry Peters referred to Gross Breesen agricultural farm as 'anti-Zionist', the historical record indicates that Gross Breesen was not actively anti-Zionist but was non-Zionist, meaning it did not teach Zionist ideology and did not train its students to emigrate to Palestine.
5. The Central Union of German Citizens of Jewish Faith (C.V.) was founded in March 1893 with the aim of combatting rising antisemitism and advocating for the social and civil rights of German Jews; it was one of the first Jewish civil rights organisations. Its focus was, according to Friesel, 'the struggle against antisemitism, especially on the political and parliamentary level' (1986, p. 123). Further analysis can be read in E. Friesel, 'The Political and Ideological Development of the Centralverein before 1914', *Leo Baeck Institute Year Book*, vol. 31, no. 1, 1986, pp. 121–146.
6. The Zionists viewed Palestine as the homeland for the Jewish people. They conceptualised a 'return' to Eretz Yisrael, their ancient land. During the period 1922 until 1948, Palestine was British Mandated Palestine. The Mandate for Palestine supported the establishment in Palestine of a 'national home for the Jewish people' (Mandate for Palestine 1922). Jewish immigration to Palestine grew exponentially as a result of Nazi persecution during the 1930s.

7. Schwarzes Fähnlein was a conservative faction of the German-Jewish youth movement. Young Jewish members were mostly upper-middle class and rejected their parents' bourgeois values. The parent organisation was the Kamaraden, which believed that life in a group or collective was preferable to individualist society. Similar to other conservative German-Jewish youth groups in Germany, Schwarzes Fähnlein was an 'élite organisation. Eighty percent of its 1300 members were university or secondary school students'. Further information can be read in C.J. Rheins, 'The Schwarzes Fähnlein, Jungenschaft 1932–1934', *The Leo Baeck Institute Year Book*, vol. 23, no. 1, 1978, pp. 173–198.
8. An in-depth discussion of German-Jewish youth movements during the Third Reich can be read in G.R. Sharfman, 'The Dilemma of German-Jewish Youths in the Third Reich: The Case of the Bund Deutsch-Jüdischer Jugend 1933–1935', *Shofar*, vol. 16, no. 3, 1998, p. 29ff.
9. The Oberschweizer was a role at Gross Breesen school, and I have given him the name Hans. The character is drawn from the recollections of Werner T. Angress in his book *Between Fear and Hope: Jewish Youth in the Third Reich*, Columbia University Press, 1988, p. 53, and Eric Baker's memoir *Sea Change* (unpublished).
10. Maria Warnke was the Pollnows' housekeeper during Hermann's early childhood when they lived at Altonaer Strasse. Harry described her as an older woman, so it could be assumed that, by the time the Pollnows moved to Schillerpromenade, Frau Warnke was too old for service.
11. It is highly unlikely that the Pollnows would have referred to Fräulein Selma by her first name. Cultural convention at this time was that housekeepers were called by their surnames. However, Fräulein Selma is referenced frequently in Harry's letter collection, specifically in 1938 and early 1939. For this reason, I have chosen to keep her name as referenced by Max Pollnow in his letters.
12. Karl Wolfskehl, *1933 A Poem Sequence*, Berlin: Schocken Books, 1947.
13. William Shakespeare, *Hamlet*, c.1599.
14. Drawn from the recollections of Eric Baker in his memoir, *Sea Change* (unpublished).
15. Ruth and Rolf Veit-Simon, Heinz and Irmgard Veit-Simon's daughter and son. Hermann was very close to the Veit-Simon children; while technically third cousins, they saw each other frequently and were more like first cousins.

16. Loebmann, Michel and Jäger were presumably regular patients of Max's.
17. Etta Veit-Simon, Heinz and Irmgard Veit-Simon's daughter.
18. The conference took place on 29–30 September 1938, among Germany, Great Britain, Italy and France. There, they signed the Munich Agreement, which concluded that Czechoslovakia would cede to Nazi Germany.
19. This recollection is taken from a separate testimony written by Harry Peters in the family collection.
20. 'Pogrom' refers to an organised attack on property and/or persons, including the murder of members of a targeted group. The November pogrom is in reference to Kristallnacht, or the Night of Broken Glass, of 9–10 November 1938. After 17-year-old Polish-Jewish Herschel Grynszpan shot German diplomat Ernst vom Rath on 7 November 1938, an eruption of anti-Semitic pogroms swept Germany, Austria and Czechoslovakia. It is known that the pogrom had been planned and the murder of vom Rath unleashed the 'spontaneous' savagery.
21. Based on the reminiscences of Ernst Cramer, in Werner Angress, *Between Fear and Hope: Jewish Youth in the Third Reich*, Columbia University Press, 1988, p. 67.
22. The Brownshirts, otherwise known as Sturmabteilung or SA, were a Nazi paramilitary group founded by Adolf Hitler in 1921, reminiscent of Mussolini's Blackshirts. They were tasked with violent intimidation of minority groups and political opposition; their presence was heavily felt at Nazi marches and rallies. By 1933, there were around two million Brownshirts, which outnumbered the German military.
23. 'Vacation' was presumably code for emigration or release from the camp. Code words and implications were frequently used in letters due to censorship and surveillance by Nazi authorities.
24. One of the few distinct recollections Harry carried with him from this period was that, when he arrived home after his imprisonment, Max remarked that at least the Nazis had given him a proper haircut; Max was always complaining the barber didn't cut Hermann's hair short enough.
25. While in his 13 September 1938 letter Max Pollnow suggests that they sold the Blüthner grand piano, Harry included the piano in the reparations document, presumably because he had forgotten his father telling him that the piano had been sold.

26. A polder is a feat of engineering mostly associated with the Netherlands, by which land is reclaimed from ocean or wetlands by forming large embankments or dikes above sea level, thereby blocking off the water, and then draining water out from the reclaimed land. Generally polders are used for agricultural purposes.
27. Gross Breesen was irrevocably changed after Kristallnacht. Bondy was no longer head educator, and most of the first and second generation of students had either emigrated or were imprisoned. Nearly the entire third generation of students perished at Auschwitz. The agricultural school continued to run until 31 August 1941, when it was closed by order of the Gestapo, and its personnel deployed to forced labour. More information can be read in Werner Angress, *Between Fear and Hope: Jewish Youth in the Third Reich*, Columbia University Press, 1988.
28. Gerald de Vahl Davis was a prominent figure in the New South Wales Jewish community. He was a member of the NSW Jewish Advisory Board and Chairman of Mutual Farms Pty Ltd, which organised Jewish immigrants to work in Australian agriculture.
29. Hanni Flaschner, Hermann's friend and fellow Gross Breesener. Presumably the Pollnows and Flaschners knew each other in Berlin.
30. A castle near Potsdam.
31. As cited in Werner Angress, *Between Fear and Hope: Jewish Youth in the Third Reich*, Columbia University Press, 1988, p. 143.
32. Scene based on a recollection from Harry Peters' papers, in a document he wrote to be included in the Gross Breesen circular letters, translated by Mithra Cox.
33. The Peninsular & Oriental Steam Navigation Company (P&O) was contracted to carry mail and had a mail service on board. Passengers were able to write and receive letters, which would be picked up and delivered at each port of call.
34. Ruth and Etta Veit-Simon, daughters of Heinz and Irmgard Veit-Simon.
35. The Murugappan 'Biloela' family is a Tamil refugee family of four who settled in Biloela, Queensland. In 2018, after the government failed to deport them due to expired visas, the family was detained on Christmas Island for two years. Public outcry ensued and after years of legal battles the family was granted permanent residency by the Albanese government in 2022.

36. 'Let's Get the Best Refugees', *The Mail* (Adelaide), 22 July 1939, p.6.
37. Gross Breeseners Klaus, Fritz, Franz, Guenther and Kurt, now Frank Jenner, James Warner, Frank Shelley, George Strong and Fred Danby, all accompanied Harry to Kuitpo Colony. George Strong remained a family friend. Erich Bacharach, who was assigned to New South Wales, had his name changed to Eric Baker.
38. Ida Forsyth, *He Came from Ireland: The Life Story of the Rev. Samuel Forsyth, O.B.E.*, Adelaide: self-published, 1952.
39. Information provided by Yad Vashem, the World Holocaust Remembrance Center, Jerusalem, www.yadvashem.org.
40. Czech for Theresienstadt.
41. Julie Wolfthorn was a German painter from a middle-class Jewish family. She was best known for portraiture and was one of the prominent women artists of the 20th century. She perished in Theresienstadt on 26 December 1944.
42. Svetlana Boym, *The Future of Nostalgia*, Basic Books, 2001, p. 175.

Acknowledgements

I would first like to acknowledge the Peramangk, Kaurna and Gundungurra people, on whose lands my grandfather's story of immigration and resettlement took place. Immigration and colonisation are inextricably linked in Australia's history, and I offer my respect to the rightful owners of these lands.

I could not have written this book without the assistance of countless people over the past four years. Most significantly, this book has stemmed from my family's experiences, knowledge, willingness to share memories, anecdotes and speculations, and the communal effort that was caring for Harry together in his final years. My family has always encouraged me to write this story and I thank them for their generosity, particularly my mother, Julia, and Harry's partner, Lynn.

I would like to thank my PhD supervisor, mentor and good friend Sue Joseph, who began this project with me back in my Honours year, six years ago. Sue has been with me since the project's nascence, back when this book was a small, unformed idea I presented to her as an uncertain undergraduate student.

Thank you to Pauline at the Adelaide Holocaust Museum for all her research help and our field trip to Kuitpo back in 2021, and to the Jewish Museum in Berlin for their clarification and assistance throughout the writing process.

Thank you to Sebastian and Gabrielle Urban and Therese Reich for their astounding efforts in translating, particularly the letter collection.

Finally, thank you to John and Heather Seymour and the National Library of Australia, who not only published my book but granted me a 2022 Summer Scholarship, which gave me access to the Library's special collections and six weeks of intensive writing time. The consistent support that the Library has given me throughout my research and, later, the publication process has made the experience of publishing my first book a true joy. Particular thanks to my editor, Brooke, and to Amelia, Lauren and Madeleine from NLA Publishing.

The National Library of Australia would like to acknowledge the vital and sustained work done by Jewish collecting and research institutions to keep safe and accessible testimonies of the Holocaust, including:

University of Southern California Shoah Foundation's survivor project, sfi.usc.edu
Leo Baeck Institute, lbi.org
Yad Vashem, the World Holocaust Remembrance Center, yadvashem.org
Adelaide Holocaust Museum, ahmsec.org.au
Jewish Museum, Berlin, jmberlin.de/en

Published by National Library of Australia Publishing
Canberra ACT 2600

ISBN: 9781922507518

The National Library of Australia acknowledges Australia's First Nations Peoples—the First Australians—as the Traditional Owners and Custodians of this land and gives respect to the Elders—past and present—and through them to all Australian Aboriginal and Torres Strait Islander people.

Publisher: Lauren Smith
Managing editor: Amelia Hartney
Editor: Brooke Lyons
Designer: Filip Bartkowiak
Image coordinator: Madeleine Warburton
Printed in China by C&C Offset Printing Co. Ltd on FSC®-certified paper.

Find out more about NLA Publishing at nla.gov.au/national-library-publishing.

A catalogue record for this book is available from the National Library of Australia